RESTORING
AMERICA'S
CONSCIENCE

RESTORING AMERICA'S CONSCIENCE

Our nation's conscience can only
be restored the way it died—
one person at a time.

By Ron Boehme

Forward by Twila Paris

Grand Rapids, Michigan 49418 USA

Restoring America's Conscience
Copyright 1996 by Ron Boehme
Published by World Publishing, Inc.
Grand Rapids, MI 49418

Cover design by JMK & Associates, Grand Rapids, MI.
Interior design by Pinpoint Marketing, Kirkland, WA.
Edited by Judy Bodmer and Heather Stroobosscher.

ISBN 0-529-106965

Library of Congress Catalog Card Number 96-60875

Printed in the United States of America

1 2 3 4 5 6 7   00 99 98 97 96

To Jason, who was
brought into this world to be
a healing force in a dark time.

May your conscience always be
sensitive and clear
toward God and men.

Table of Contents

Foreword

By Twila Paris

FOR SOME YEARS I've been concerned about the moral decay in our society. Things aren't the way they used to be.

I grew up in rural, northwest Arkansas, sheltered from many of the problems people face in our cities. Life was slow-paced, you knew almost everyone in town, and good values were a part of the culture. You didn't have to think much about right and wrong. Everybody went to church and lived the golden rule.

Traveling around the country the past few years in music ministry awakened me to how far our country has slipped. Much of this cultural erosion burst upon us in the past few years. Crime has exploded, many of our nation's kids now come from broken homes, and the whole moral landscape seems to be spinning out of control.

At concerts, I've witnessed firsthand the spiritual hunger of young people for a way of life that has vanished. This motivated me to write songs encouraging people to love God, do what's right, and believe that our nation can be changed for the good.

Now I've read a book that shares that desire and points the way back. It's written by Ron Boehme, who's been with Youth With A Mission for many years.

I met Ron when I was growing up as a kid in the Youth With A Mission ministry center in northwest Arkansas where my father, Oren, is the director. Ron visited our community on various occasions speaking to discipleship schools and attending different conferences. Like many YWAM leaders, he had a love for truth and a clear message of wholehearted devotion to God that impacted my life.

Recently, Ron showed me a preview of his newest book, *Restoring America's Conscience*. Between rehearsals and preparations for an upcoming concert tour, I read through it.

The book confirmed many things. It helped me understand why our country has gone down hill so suddenly—we didn't listen to that precious voice of conscience inside. It also gave practical steps on how to clear my conscience and treat it as a treasure.

I was also really challenged, especially as I took the Freedom Train journey through the different conscience stops we all encounter in our lives. Each one dealt with real down-to-earth situations we all commonly face. It was easy reading, but also very convicting—and freeing. The Lord spoke to my heart, and I made commitments to change a few things.

Mostly, the book motivated me to increase the intensity of my witness in the realm God has placed me. Music is a powerful medium that has brought much darkness and moral confusion to America. It's an industry filled with much dirtiness and manipulation. But it also has great potential to beam God's truth into the hearts of millions.

Ron's book is a wake up call to people of faith. It reminds us that God wants all of us to be a part of the spiritual and moral transformation of our world. Now I'm more convinced than ever that we can do it together with hearts that are sensitive to Him.

I strongly encourage you to read this book, pray over it, and ask God for the power to live its truth in our darkening world. Together we can turn on the light. Our conscience is the light switch. God is the power source.

If enough of us flick on the switches, the enemy will have to flee.

Not a bad idea. Start reading!

Acknowledgments

I WOULD LIKE to thank Bill Gothard and Winkie Pratney for their excellent writings and teachings on having a clear and sensitive conscience. They originally opened my eyes to this important dimension of my life.

The writings of nineteenth-century evangelist Charles Finney have been my greatest influence. Much of the content of this book comes from Finney's letters and sermons.

Special thanks are due to Lois Walfrid Johnson for encouraging me to do this book. Shirley Walston, Scott Pinzon, and Judy Bodmer have been fine editors who have made the truth clear. Many thanks to numerous YWAM intercessors who prayed this project through. And finally, I'm most grateful to my wife, Shirley, and our six children for encouraging me as I labored away on the computer for days at a time.

RESTORING
AMERICA'S
CONSCIENCE

Introduction

ONE PRIVILEGE OF speaking around the world is running into people you've met in other places.

A few years ago I began to notice an interesting pattern. Though I speak at churches, schools, or conferences on a variety of subjects, more often than not when I meet former students, they tell me the greatest impact I made on their life was my teaching on conscience.

I didn't think this subject was the most exciting material I shared, yet it was the material they remembered for years. Sometimes they didn't remember my name, but they never forgot the teaching on the importance of a good conscience.

It finally sunk in that this subject was so vital I needed to put it into book form for larger distribution. The following is my attempt to be obedient.

The Bible and common usage differentiate between two aspects of conscience. One is individual conscience where relative freedom of conviction and variety are both allowed and treasured (1 Corinthians 10:27–30). The other is general conscience—or knowledge of unchanging right and wrong—to which God holds all of us accountable (Romans 1:18–32).

This book focuses on the breakdown of general conscience in the United States. Our civilization is dying due to its loss of a moral compass. That awakening begins with you and me as we open our hearts to "turn from [our] evil ways" (2 Chronicles 7:14).

I am consciously blowing a trumpet of surrender to personal holiness, not creating another guilt ridden legalistic system that will frustrate those who want to please God. Our conscience regulates our attitudes and actions. If we're to see revival, we must expose both empty liberal behavior and mean spirited legalism.

I also discovered during my research that the definition of general conscience has changed in the past few decades. Prior to the modern era, conscience was uniformly recognized as the God-given ability to know right from wrong; that is, "some requirements found in Moses' Teachings are written in their hearts. Their consciences speak to them. Their thoughts accuse them on one occasion and defend them on another" (Romans 2:15). Recently, however, popular psychology has dropped the God-origin of conscience and redefined it as whatever one believes about right and wrong.

I adhere to the traditional-historical definition of conscience and chalk up its impostor to the consequences of modern man attempting to relativize truth via a dull conscience. Chuck Colson is right when he says that our conscience is God-given—it only needs to be nurtured. This book assumes that biblical-historical premise.

I hope this book impacts your own heart and life. Take the time to dig into the questions at the end of each chapter and do your personal homework. After that, it might be helpful to get a group of friends together to study and apply the material.

May the truths on these pages help you to awaken and protect the priceless gift of conscience that God has given you. Years from now it won't matter if you remember me. What you do with your conscience toward God and others is the important thing.

Don't forget. And pass it on.

SECTION ONE

Conscience in America

*"Labor to keep alive in your breast that little
spark of celestial fire called conscience."*[1]

—*George Washington*

CHAPTER 1

An Awakening of Conscience

I'D BEEN SITTING, pacing, praying, and crying for almost five hours. It was the fall of 1974, and I'd holed up in the quiet of my grandparents' home overlooking Puget Sound in Washington state to do some serious business with God. Recently, I'd read a book that encouraged me to clean up my heart and life from the sins of my past. This was not my conversion day, but a time of honesty and obedience following my commitment to Christ years earlier.

The book I was reading, *Revival Lectures* by Charles Finney, gave clear instructions about how I could free myself from past wrongs. Who wouldn't want that? Its message was straightforward and challenging: I needed to list all my past sins, make things right with God and others, and then keep my conscience clear for the rest of my life (Proverbs 28:13).

At twenty-one, I'd committed enough youthful sins to keep me busy for a while.

Plopping down my athletic, six-foot frame at the kitchen table, I listed on paper every sin I remembered committing. It's a good thing I couldn't recall them all because that probably would have killed me. After five hours of soul-searching, my stack of scribbled papers contained hundreds of notations of wrongs I'd done to God and others in my short life.

The list included my foul mouth in junior high, a struggle with lust and pornography as a teenager, and some years of rebellion toward my parents. There were the sins of anger, jealousy, envy, and pride that hurt others in relationships I used for selfish advantage. Most of all, though raised in church, I'd shut God out of the center of my attitudes and values. I'd lived for self and its empty pleasures.

All of these sins had numbed me for years. They'd produced confusion, insecurity, purposelessness, and a lack of power. In friendships, I was guarded, keeping things on a shallow plane to keep from getting hurt. Sexual lust was a constant temptation and gnawing daydream.

A final time I asked the Lord to show me areas of my darkened conscience that needed to be confessed, made right, and restored. This time the words came clearly to my heart: "There is nothing more." With tears streaming down my cheeks, I went into the living room. There I prayed, worshipped, and burned in the fireplace the record of wrongs that had crippled my life for years.

From that day forth, I determined to live my life with a clear conscience before God and men. I knew I wasn't suddenly perfect now. Obviously, there would be more sins to confess, more understanding to gain, and deeper workings of the Holy Spirit throughout my lifetime.

For the first time I knew the freedom and power of a clean conscience. Though Jesus had forgiven my sins when I accepted him as my Savior years before, I'd never allowed him to break the power of sin through awakening my conscience. At the end of this day, I thanked God for cleansing my conscience and asked him to help me keep it sensitive from then on.

Paul's Awakening of Conscience

The Apostle Paul had a profound awakening of conscience as a young man. Though zealously religious, he rejected the claims of Jesus and persecuted Christians. While on the road to Damascus, God invaded Paul's comfort zone and awakened his heart and mind. These were Jesus' words to him: "'Saul, Saul, why do you persecute me? It's hard for you to kick against the goads'" (Acts 26:14 NIV).

A goad was a sharp, pointed stick that Hebrew farmers used to keep their oxen plowing in a straight line. Whenever an ox veered off his path while plowing the soil, this painful little instrument jabbed into the ox's side reminding it to get back in line. Each time it wandered off, it got another jab.

Paul was doing the same thing with his conscience. Instead of allowing it to guide him in the right way, he'd allowed it to be a painful goad that smarted every time he did wrong. Jesus' loving advice to him was to stop stabbing himself and enter into a life of freedom and peace.

Paul abruptly changed his life, put his trust in Jesus, and became a great spiritual leader. Toward the end of his life, he could boldly say, ". . . I always do my best to have a clear conscience in the sight of God and people" (Acts 24:16).

Our conscience can be a friendly guide along life's pathway, or it can be a very painful goad. The choice is ours. That's God's original design.

God's Sound—Our Speaker

The conscience is a part of the human personality. Closely related to the will and emotions, it is the ability of the mind to confirm and enforce right and wrong behavior. Romans 2:15 describes the human conscience this way:

> ". . . in their hearts they know right from wrong. God's laws are written within them; their own conscience accuses them, or sometimes excuses them." (Living Bible)

Conscience is a God-given sense of right and wrong written in every heart. It's being able to know what's true, coupled with right feeling toward obedience and wrong feeling toward disobedience.

This ability to confirm and enforce right and wrong behavior is a precious gift from God. Without it, we would find ourselves drifting along in a world of confusing options. A mind without a conscience would be like a body without nerves. If you smashed your finger with a hammer and felt no pain, you might continue hitting it, not knowing the severe damage you were doing.

The conscience does that and more. It not only pains you when you choose to go against it, but it tells you the right thing to do before you do the smashing. It guides before you choose and registers approval or disapproval after the action. That's pretty amazing!

But the human conscience can also be extremely perverted or darkened. It can be "bent" to acknowledge the wrong things or deadened to hear nothing at all. It's a moldable part of our spiritual life that must be kept clean, sensitive, and anchored to God's Word.

Noah Webster, the author of the original 1828 *Webster's Dictionary*, agreed with the long held historical definition of conscience as the "judgment of right and wrong, or the faculty, power or principle within us, which decides on the lawfulness or unlawfulness of our own actions and affections and instantly approves or condemns them. Conscience is called by some writers the moral sense."[2]

Chuck Colson, the famous convert of Watergate and now president of Prison Fellowship says it this way:

> Where does conscience come from? It's something
> God gives us at birth, but it has to be cultivated.[3]

This divinely planted sense of right and wrong is easily warped or perverted. But when our conscience is open to God's truth, it acts like a "judge" inside us. When we do right, according to God's standards and principles, our conscience "smiles" upon our action. We feel approval and encouragement. But when we do wrong, our conscience "frowns" upon our wrong choice, and we feel guilty, confused, or wrong.

In some ways, your conscience is like a stereo speaker. If the speaker is well built, with wires properly connected to the sound system, the sound it produces will be clear and understandable. But if you abuse the speaker or the wires get frayed, then the sound will be fuzzy, faint, or fail to get through at all.

When this happens, the sound system is not at fault. Its pitch and clarity have not changed. The problem is the speaker not receiving the clear signal.

Our children have a small boom box that illustrates this point. When they first received it a few Christmases ago, its sound was powerful and clear. Sometimes they'd turn it up so loud in their room that the whole upstairs would shake!

After it got dropped a few times, dragged around, and the volume turned up too high, its sound became muffled and distorted. Because the speakers weren't properly taken care of, this Christmas, their stereo needs to be replaced.

The same is true of our consciences. If we do not protect and cherish our God-given conscience, then the truth about what's right and wrong becomes fuzzy, barely discernible, or completely silent. God's beam of truth hasn't changed. His signal is still as clear as it has always been. But our speaker—the human conscience—has been abused in a way that does not allow it to function properly.

It's crucial to listen to your conscience. The more you disobey it, the harder it is to hear. If you disobey it often enough, it won't direct you in the right way but will become clouded by deception. But if you let your God-given conscience guide you—according to God's Word—it will not let you down. Freedom and success will be yours.

Conscience in the Bible

The word "conscience" (translated from the Greek word *suneidesis* [soon-i'-day-sis], meaning moral consciousness or conscience), occurs about thirty times throughout the Scriptures. However, the Bible uses many other words, such as the heart, mind, and spirit, to discuss the importance of knowing right from wrong. Taken together, conscience is a large Bible topic. A few examples:

- When Jesus forgave the woman caught in adultery, the people who wanted to stone her were convicted in their consciences and left one by one, leaving Jesus alone with the woman (John 8:9).

- Twice in the book of Acts, Paul mentions the importance of maintaining a good conscience before God and men (Acts 23:1 and 24:16).

- In his letter to the Romans, Paul mentions conscience three times, once in his own testimony (Romans 9:1) and twice in exhorting the Roman believers to live holy lives (Romans 2:15 and 13:5).

- To the immature Corinthian believers, Paul brought up the subject of conscience eleven times in many different contexts. There was a big need in Corinth for teaching on conscience. Here are a couple of references:

> We are proud that our conscience is clear. We are proud of the way we have lived in this world. We have lived with a God-given holiness and sincerity, especially toward you. . . . (2 Corinthians 1:12)

> Rather, we have renounced secret and shameful ways; we do not use deception, nor do we distort the word of God. On the contrary, by setting forth the truth plainly we commend ourselves

to every man's conscience in the sight of God.
(2 Corinthians 4:2-3 NIV)

- The book of Hebrews contains five references to the importance of a good conscience. We are to allow Christ to "cleanse our consciences from the useless things we have done" (Hebrews 9:14). We are also encouraged to "draw near to God with a sincere heart in full assurance of faith, having our hearts sprinkled to cleanse us from a guilty conscience and having our bodies washed with pure water" (Hebrews 10:22 NIV).

- Peter mentions the importance of a clear conscience three times in his letters. In 1 Peter 3:15–16 he says:

   But dedicate your lives to Christ as Lord. Always be ready to defend your confidence in God when anyone asks you to explain it. However, make your defense with gentleness and respect. Keep your conscience clear . . .

- In the same chapter, he compares the act of baptism to having a good conscience:

   Baptism . . . now saves you. Baptism doesn't save by removing dirt from the body. Rather, baptism is a request to God for a clear conscience. It saves you through Jesus Christ, who came back from death to life. (1 Peter 3:21)

A Spiritual Father's Advice

Perhaps the Bible's clearest teaching on conscience is found in Paul's two letters to his spiritual son Timothy. Five times, in the space of two letters, he mentions to Timothy the importance of having a good conscience. Let's look at four of those references.

Number One

Paul opens his first letter with this blockbuster perspective on Christian maturity:

> My goal in giving you this order is for love to flow from a pure heart, from a clear conscience, and from a sincere faith. (1 Timothy 1:5)

In all of our life-situations, God wants us to respond as loving people (this brings to mind the words of Jesus in John 13:34–35). We achieve this life of love by possessing three things: a pure heart, a good conscience, and a sincere faith.

A good conscience is a crucial part of this maturity triad. If you want a strong foundation, use a good conscience as a pillar to build on.

Number Two

In 1 Timothy 1:18–20, Paul warns us about the consequences of a bad conscience:

> Timothy, my child, I'm giving you this order about the prophecies that are still coming to you: Use these prophecies in faith and with a clear conscience to fight this noble war. Some have refused to let their

faith guide their conscience and their faith has been destroyed like a wrecked ship. Among these people are Hymenaeus and Alexander, whom I have handed over to Satan in order to teach them not to dishonor God.

Paul warns Timothy that Christian soldiers win the fight through faith and a good conscience. If these things are not maintained, then a person's spiritual life can go on the rocks.

Hymenaeus and Alexander have done just that and are under judgment. Paul warns not to be like them but to fight life's battles with faith and a good conscience.

Number Three

First Timothy 3 contains qualifications for leadership in the Body of Christ:

> Deacons must also be of good character. They must not be two-faced or addicted to alcohol. They must not use shameful ways to make money. They must have clear consciences about possessing the mystery of the Christian faith. (1 Timothy 3:8–10)

Paul knew the future of the Church depended on the purity of its leaders. They cannot be a models for others if their own lives are shady or gray. That truth brings to mind a recent tragedy in my own hometown.

Father Fred Aylward moved into Port Orchard, Washington, in the early 1990s and started an orthodox Catholic Church. He was a large, jovial man who reminded me of Friar Tuck in the story of *Robin Hood*. To support himself while he built his parish, he ran a small printing business on the side. Eventually we began taking all our printing needs to him.

A year ago, he personally renovated the Blessed Margaret sanctuary to accommodate 150 worshippers. The work was booming.

"Father Fred," who drove a red sports car, was a respected leader in the town. Two months ago, his sports car was found wrecked in a deep ravine. There was no sign of Fred and his ten-year-old granddaughter whom he'd picked up that afternoon. Two days later, the priest was arrested in California on kidnapping charges. He'd faked the accident to skip town, intending to relocate in South America. Soon the truth came out that he'd been molesting the girl for years. He'd also been seeing a local prostitute, forging papers for drug dealers, and embezzling thousands of dollars from the church.

Our town is still in shock from the sin of this phony spiritual leader. It will take years for trust to be restored.

Number Four

Paul's fourth reference to conscience is his own personal testimony:

> I constantly remember you in my prayers night and day when I thank God, whom I serve with a clear conscience as my ancestors did. (2 Timothy 1:3)

Paul goes on to mention Timothy's grandmother, Lois, and mother, Eunice, who were examples to Timothy of the same faith. This faith was rooted by a clear conscience. It was a key to Paul's personal life and success.

The importance of a good conscience was so important to Paul he mentioned it continually. He also understood the biblical truth that our most important possessions are internal, not external. They are inside us and need to be cherished above everything else.

Our Internal Property

My conscience—a valuable inner property? What are you talking about?

When we use the word "property," a little definition card goes up in our mind that says property consists of land, homes, and cars. They are material assets that we own or have worked for.

But a few generations back, this material definition of property was partial at best. Yes, external things were a part of a man's property, but they were not the whole or even the most important.

In early America, people understood that human beings possessed internal and external properties. This biblical distinction was clearly expounded in the writings of John Locke, William Blackstone, and other post-Reformation thinkers whose writings greatly impacted many of our founding fathers.[4]

External property included their houses, businesses, and livestock. Far more important were their internal possessions like the heart and its affections, the mind and its thoughts, and the conscience and its convictions.

Rob a man's home and you were considered a thief. A man had a right to material possessions, and taking them was considered a crime. But robbing a man's heart or conscience of his convictions was even worse. It was a violation of his inner property. That was considered tyranny.

This was really the essence of the American revolution. Great Britain didn't have the right to violate the inner convictions of the American people. They were "endowed by their Creator with certain unalienable rights. Among these rights were life, liberty, and the pursuit of happiness."

Samuel Adams, a great Revolutionary leader, said:

> Among the natural rights of the Colonists are these: First a right to life; Secondly, to liberty; Thirdly, to property; . . . Every man living in or out of a state of civil society has a right to peaceably and quietly worship God according to the dictates of his conscience.[5]

This was the reason the Pilgrims and others came to America. In England, their internal property—including the right to conscience and the worship of God—had been ransacked. They came to these shores to again take possession of their convictions. Central to these internal possessions was a conscience that yearned to worship God in liberty and purity.

No one articulated the supreme value of the human conscience more clearly than our nation's fourth president, James Madison, writing about property:

> . . . In the former sense, a man's land, or merchandise or money, is called his property. In the latter sense, a man has a property in his opinions and the free communication of them. He has a property of

peculiar value in his religious opinions, and in the
profession and practice dictated by them....
Government is instituted to protect property of
every sort . . . this being the end of government.
Conscience is the most sacred of all property.[6]

"The Most Sacred Of All Property"

What a "revolutionary" idea. If we cherish and guard
our conscience, it will lead us into truth that brings life and
blessing. But if we allow our conscience to be trampled upon,
then we can lose our life and liberty. Even worse, we can lose
our soul.

Isn't this Jesus' point in the story of the rich man found
in Luke 12:15–21? He built bigger and bigger barns, thinking he was secure in his external possessions. But he neglected his inner being and its state before his Creator. God's
sobering words to him were, "I will demand your life from
you tonight!"

He thought he had everything, but in reality he really
had nothing of eternal value.

It's one thing to lose all your material possessions. It happened to Job, but he still clung to his faith in God. If you allow
your conscience to be stolen or defiled, you can lose not only the
blessings of this life but also the privileges of the one to come.

For hundreds of years, many Americans read their Bibles
and understood the importance of maintaining a good conscience. This obedience produced a strong society whose
family life, crime levels, and social arenas were relatively
stable and predictable from the 1730s to the 1940s. With

a few exceptions, America was a secure and moral nation for eleven generations.

The past two generations have failed to let their conscience be their guide. Instead, a crippled conscience has become a painful goad that torments the nation daily with apathy, loneliness, and guilt. This lack of the fear of God has helped produce a massive crime wave, many broken relationships, and a society being consumed by violence and death.

Awakening A Nation

One hundred seventy-five years ago, America was going through another time of national decline. Onto the stage of history walked a man whose book *Revival Lectures* changed my life.

Charles Finney was a real American hero. Born in Warren, Connecticut, in 1792, he trained to be a lawyer. Following his conversion to Christ at twenty-nine, he launched a successful career as an evangelist, author, and college professor. In the 1820s and 1830s, powerful revivals followed his ministry. As Christ's advocate, he laid bare the hearts and consciences of men and women with the Law of God and Gospel of Christ. In some meetings, people shook with fear as he clearly exposed their sins in the light of the Scriptures.

Finney awakened the conscience of America by proclaiming God's eternal truth. Businessmen, professors, doctors, lawyers—people from all walks of life—came to hear this impassioned preacher who appealed to their minds and emotions.

After two exhausting decades of ministry, Finney cruised the Mediterranean to regain his failing health. Thinking he might die, he returned to New York and delivered a series of messages that were published in 1834 as *Lectures on Revivals of Religion*. Amazingly, he lived forty-one more years after he wrote them.

Finney preached a message of changed hearts and lives through a conscience that was awakened to God. He was on the forefront of the antislavery movement, and helped found Oberlin College, a prominent gathering place for anti-slavery coalitions.

Of the hundreds of thousands who became Christians under his ministry, it's estimated that seventy to eighty percent stayed true to their conversion. In today's evangelistic crusades, under ten percent of those who make decisions follow Christ for a lifetime. His secret?

The depth and clarity of the message. He appealed to people's consciences, then led them to the cross.

A recent article in *Reader's Digest* entitled "Our Kindest City" describes the affect of Finney's ministry on Rochester, New York, almost 150 years after his last visit:

> Finney spent six months in Rochester and con-verted hundreds of residents. He scorched their consciences and urged them not to follow the self-ish ways of the world . . . The influence of Finney's powerful message is still felt in Rochester because it was passed down in so many different ways. Parents who heard the evangelist told their chil-dren. Ministers and Sunday school teachers carried the word to their flocks. And generation after

generation of Rochesterians stayed in the city and preserved the Finney legacy.[7]

According to the article in *Reader's Digest,* Rochester is today considered America's kindest city. All because one man awakened the conscience of his converts to reject sin and make Jesus the Lord of their lives. There was no easy-believism or partial Lordship. Either Jesus was Lord of all, or he wasn't Lord at all.

A Lesson From History

In the nineteenth century, America was going through incredible changes as a nation. The new country, born in a time of revival and forged through the bloodshed and travail of the Revolutionary War, catapulted onto the world scene as a new emerging power:

- The map changed as the nation stretched to encompass its natural borders from Atlantic to Pacific.

- The economy changed as people streamed into factories and the newly born industrial sector.

- Family life changed as people left their farms, loaded belongings on wagon trains, and moved west.

- Faith changed as dependence on God was replaced with an independent pioneer spirit. Although it denied God, the philosophy of evolution became popular when Charles Darwin's book *Origin of Species* was published in 1858.

By mid-century, with the Civil War looming, America was deeply divided, troubled in conscience and soul. In 1859 the stock market crashed bringing further anxiety. War now seemed inevitable as states began to secede from the Union.

It was into this state of deepening darkness that Charles Finney and others appealed to the hearts of men and women. America needed a wake-up call. And it needed to begin with a renewal of private and public conscience before a Holy God.

As public morals worsened, Mr. Finney sounded the trumpet of alarm. The conscience of America needed awakening. Read carefully his prophetic words:

> I believe it is a fact generally admitted that there is much less conscience manifested by men and women in nearly all walks of life than there was forty years ago. There is justly much complaint of this, and there seems to be but little prospect of reformation. The rings and frauds and villainies in high and low places, among all ranks of men, are most alarming, and one is almost compelled to ask: "Can anybody be safely trusted?"

Doesn't that sound familiar? Notice where Mr. Finney placed the blame:

> Now what is the cause of this degeneracy? Doubtless there are many causes that contribute more or less directly to it, but I am persuaded that the fault is more in the ministry and public press than in any

and all things else. Ministers have ceased in great measure to probe the consciences of men with the spiritual law of God. So far as my knowledge extends, there has been a great letting down and ignoring the searching claims of God's law as revealed in His Word. This law is the only standard of true morality. "By the law is the knowledge of sin." The law is the quickener of the human conscience. Just in proportion as the spirituality of God's law is kept out of view there will be manifest a decay of conscience. This must be the inevitable result.[8]

Quite a picture, isn't it? Over a forty year period—just one generation—Mr. Finney lamented that the consciences of the American people had radically changed. This led to a breakdown of trust in every aspect of society. Who had failed?

First, the Christian leaders of the day. They were not preaching the truth about sin and lifting up God's Law as the only basis of a safe and civil society.

Secondly, the press wasn't helping either. Instead of encouraging public virtue and morality, the media outlets were filling the nation with trash and filth. Liquor ads stood where sermons had once been published. Tobacco smoking and chewing were touted as preferred social graces.

The result: a decay of conscience. As tooth decay rots the teeth and often leads to their removal, the decay of conscience in people's lives was rotting the nation.

Something needed to be done.

Charles Finney's final blast accused pastors of not declaring truth from the pulpit. In Judeo-Christian America, the spiritual leaders of the day had let darkness put out the light:

If there is a decay of conscience, the pulpit is responsible for it. If the public press lacks moral dis-
crimination, the pulpit is responsible for it. If the
Church is degenerate and worldly, the pulpit is
responsible for it. If the world loses its interest in
religion (Christianity), the pulpit is responsible for
it. If Satan rules in our halls of legislation, the pulpit is responsible for it. If our politics become so
corrupt that the very foundations of our government are ready to fall away, the pulpit is responsible for it. Let us not ignore this fact my dear
brethren; but let us lay it to heart and be thoroughly awake to our responsibility in respect to
the morals of this nation.[9]

The Great Revival

On October 14, 1857, the nation staggered under a
stock market crash. Financial panic followed. Soon prayer
meetings sprang up all over the nation at noon and on
Sundays. Thousands were coming to pray. Jeremiah
Lanphier's famous Fulton Street prayer meeting in New York
City grew from six people in October to over three thousand
within three months. By spring, ten thousand businessmen
were meeting daily in New York City for prayer.

By January of 1858, newspapers were sending reporters
to cover the prayer meetings. In Massachusetts, where Charles
Finney was preaching, over five thousand conversions took
place before the end of March. Newspapers everywhere made
the revival front page news. New Haven, Connecticut: "City's

Biggest Church Packed Twice Daily for Prayer." Albany, New York: "State Legislators Get Down on Knees." Washington, D.C.: "Five Prayer Meetings Go Round the Clock."

In Chicago, where two thousand showed up for prayer in the Metropolitan Theater, a newspaper commented:

> So far as the effects of the present religious movement are concerned, they are apparent to all. The merchant, the farmer, the mechanic—all who have been within their influence—have been incited to better things; to a more orderly and honest way of life. All have been more or less influenced by this excitement.[10]

As prayer deepened and pastors proclaimed God's truth, great revival swept across the nation. At its peak, in 1858, estimates claim over fifty thousand people were giving their lives to Christ each week in the United States.[11]

The awakening continued. It's estimated that three hundred thousand to one million people returned to the faith of their fathers between 1857 and 1858.[12] Were it not for the start of the Civil War, there's no telling how long the revival would have lasted. Even during the War, God continued to pour out his Spirit upon the troubled and divided nation. Over 150,000 Confederate soldiers became Christians.

This awakening of the American heart and conscience became known in history as the Great Revival. It did not stop the Civil War. (According to Abraham Lincoln, that was God's necessary punishment for the sin of slavery.) Nor did it solve all of the nation's problems. Yet one of its fruits was the abolition of slavery, the greatest conscience issue of the day. It also restored, along with the war, a sense of public and private morality to a nation in decay.

The Great Revival came to America during the darkest moment of her young history. It was also America's last full-blown revival.

Can It Happen Again?

We, too, live in a world of incredible changes.

- The world map changes daily after the fall of the Iron Curtain, nationalistic infighting, and the emergence of developing countries.

- The economies of the West teeter on the edge of recession and depression. They are also linked together in a global expansion of trade and opportunity.

- Families are torn apart by a highly mobile society, single parent homes, working moms and dads which is causing major child neglect, and a crumbling social fabric.

- Faith in the God of the Bible has been replaced by a myriad of gods, philosophies, and religious expressions. Atheism reigns in our public institutions.

If a spiritual awakening of conscience was needed in the 1800s, then it is desperately needed today. If Charles Finney and his contemporaries could visit America today, they would be appalled at the present state of our nation.

America today is far worse than America was in 1857. Divorce, substance abuse, child abuse, homicides, family break-down, violent crime, immorality, pornographic distribution, abortion, infanticide, and numerous other societal ills have all reached epic proportions. We have experienced an unprece-dented decay of conscience that has brought us to a point of danger and despair.

We desperately need God to do it again. Our hearts need to change and the blinders must be taken off our eyes. New life begins when God opens our eyes and awakens our consciences to his unaltered truth. His standards have never changed. We are the ones who have floated off into fantasy and error.

That awakening begins with you and me.

Will you allow your heart to be made sensitive to God? Are you willing to have your conscience awakened by the blazing clarity of his Word and commands?

God wants you to live a clean and victorious life in the midst of an ever darkening world. If you will follow his lead, the following promise applies to you:

> Arise! Shine! Your light has come, and the glory of
> the LORD has dawned. Darkness now covers the
> earth, and thick darkness covers the nations. But the
> LORD dawns, and his glory appears over you.
> Nations will come to your light, and kings will come
> to the brightness of your dawn. (Isaiah 60:1–3)

Your conscience is the key. Without its renewal, you will never overcome the thickening darkness of a world in cultural decay.

In the next chapter we'll explore the unprecedented moral free fall of the United States at the end of the twentieth century.

For Thought, Discussion, and Action

1. Is your conscience clear before God and others? Have you taken the time to let God search the inner recesses of your heart? Explain.

2. Define the human conscience. What are its two primary functions? Explain how it can be either a loving guide or a painful goad.

3. Are all people's consciences the same? What determines our ability to hear God's voice in our conscience? Explain how our conscience is similar to a stereo speaker.

4. Which of Paul's words to Timothy on the subject of conscience really stand out to you? Explain. Why is a clear conscience a basic qualification for leaders in the Church.

5. Why is conscience the most sacred of all property? Do we consider it important today? In what ways does our society defile people's consciences?

6. How does America in the last century compare with the America of today? Were there higher standards of morality one hundred years ago? Why or why not?

7. Make your conscience your prize possession. Cherish it. Be willing, like our ancestors, to live and die for freedom of conscience under God.

CHAPTER 2

Decay of Conscience

"We are witnessing in America the most terrifying thing that could happen to a society—the death of conscience."[1]   —*Chuck Colson*

PEOPLE HURRIED TO their seats. The curtain was rising at the Bijou Theater in Your Town, Your State, USA. Jack and Jane American quickly purchased their fifteen-cent tickets for the Saturday afternoon matinee and plopped down excitedly to watch the show. It was 1939. Big screen movies were the marvel of the day, and this show had the entire country buzzing.

Gone With the Wind relived the pain and agony of the nation during the tragic Civil War. In piercing silence, the small-town audience gazed upon the wonder of film retelling the epic drama.

Near the end, Clark Gable, the hero of Hollywood for nearly thirty years, turned to Vivian Leigh and in a moment of passion expanded the boundaries of public decency with one little word: "Damn!"

Jack and Jane gasped. Around them, townspeople blushed and nervously looked at each other.

For the first time in decades, profanity was displayed by a mainstream American medium—the movie house. It hit the American heart and mind like a boulder. Many angrily left the theater that day wondering what was happening in America. A former state senator friend of mine said that her parents wouldn't let her see the movie because of the public profanity.

Little did anyone know just how far the national conscience would sink into the abyss of decay.

We've Come A Long Way

Some today would laugh at what people were sensitive to fifty years ago. One small swear word. Hey, what's the big deal?

Well, in 1939 it was a big deal. For eighty years American culture lived off the good fruits of the last Great Revival. There were some seasons of backsliding, but after two world wars and the Great Depression, America still maintained fairly high standards of virtue in private and public morality.

These virtues began to recede from public consciousness following World War II. Another war—a spiritual and moral one—followed. It aimed at the heart and soul of the United States of America.

"Righteousness lifts up a nation," says Proverbs 14:34. For nearly two hundred years, America rose in leadership among the nations of the world. As the great historian Alexis de Tocqueville observed in 1820, "America is great because America is good. And once America loses her goodness, she will cease to be great." [2]

The 1940s and 50s saw the gradual loosening of a national Christian conscience that had been stable for nearly two hundred years. The big invasion began in the 1960s. Today, our nation has plummeted into *a mind-boggling decay of conscience that has nearly destroyed our social fabric.*

The War On Good

The Vietnam War was not America's biggest defeat. A cultural war of the past generation has done far more damage to the fabric of our nation than any military loss. Spiritual forces of darkness, such as Paul mentions in Ephesians 6:12, have unleashed a filthiness into our public soul that has nearly destroyed an entire culture.

Recently two brothers were acquitted of murdering their parents. They shot them in the back while the parents ate popcorn and watched a movie. When their mother didn't die immediately, one brother reloaded and shot her in the face.

The week before, a woman was acquitted of cutting off her husband's penis. Attacking him with a knife after he allegedly forced her to have sex, she completely severed his sexual organ without guilt or remorse. The jury concurred that she was a victim, not a criminal.

Every night the evening news almost casually mentions murders, rapes, arsons, thefts, and myriads of other examples of the abandonment of conscience in our nation. Fifty years ago our consciences were awake and sensitive to right and wrong. We knew how to blush. We knew how to weep. People knew what was good, and they knew what was wrong.

Let's look for a moment at five elements of spiritual and moral warfare that have killed the American conscience. These tactical strategies are also found in most human wars. The devil himself started this war in an attempt to destroy the greatness of the United States. John 10:10 tells us, "A thief comes only to steal, kill, and destroy. . . ."

Tactic One: Divide and Conquer

For 150 years, Americans highly valued the institution of marriage. Divorce was rare and usually viewed with contempt. Since 1960, divorce has increased almost two hundred percent. Now nearly one in two first marriages ends in divorce.[3] No-fault divorce has removed blame, so marriage is now viewed as a convenience, not as a binding contract. The results, especially on children, have been devastating.

Last week I visited a friend who is dying of AIDS. He grew up in a broken home where his dad divorced his mom and abandoned him. After struggling for years with a dominant mother and the hurt associated with an absent father, he fled into a homosexual lifestyle where he contracted the HIV virus. Now Tom will be dead before he reaches forty, a victim of divorce and his own improper response.[4]

Tactic Two: Moral Subversion

In one full generation, America has departed from a broad based and relatively stable moral consensus to every imaginable form of sexual perversion. Various forms of pornography are now featured in our grocery stores. R- and X-rated movies, cable television, and video outlets as numerous as fast food restaurants daily spew into our homes the garbage of illicit sex, fashionable affairs, adultery, homosexuality, bestiality, and every imaginable perversion.

Is it any wonder that the past two decades have produced twenty new venereal diseases, sixteen percent of the U.S. population is suffering from herpes, and syphilis is at a forty-year high with 134,000 new infections per year?[5]

Recent studies by *Focus on the Family* show that eighty percent of boys and seventy percent of girls are no longer virgins by the age of eighteen. Teen pregnancies have doubled in the past two decades. About three million teenagers each year contract a sexually transmitted disease due to their morally dirty lifestyle.[6]

The drive to legitimatize homosexuality, the final destination of a sexually perverted society, is ample evidence of a crumbling culture. Homosexual sin, by its very nature, is twisted, unnatural and psychologically damaging. Its increasing acceptance reveals the depths of perversion to which America has sunk.

David Wilkerson, author of *The Cross and the Switchblade*, says that for three decades, a demonic host of unclean spirits has flooded the American nation with unrestrained sexual filth.[7] We are paying deeply as a people for this subversion of conscience. It is a price that will not only be paid by us, but by our great-grandchildren.

Tactic Three: Chemical Warfare

As in the decline of the last century, our era shows a revival of alcoholic consumption. Over ten million Americans are alcoholics. They account for over fifty percent of all the fatalities that occur on our nation's highways.[8]

Drugs are the "candy" of a nation living for substance thrills. There are nearly two million cocaine users in the U.S. Ninety percent of graduating seniors have used illicit alcohol or drugs on at least one occasion.[9] Though drug use has stabilized since the 1980s, it is still a primary reason for inner city crime.

Tactic Four: Propaganda and Lies

To win a spiritual war, you need to capture the battlefield of the mind. In a nation, this means controlling the education system that molds the up-and-coming generation.

The public schools have declined in America for three decades. SAT scores have dropped nearly eighty points, though school spending has increased significantly. While TV watching has increased two hours more per day since the 1960s, literacy has plummeted.[10]

Another concern is the growing power of the American media, which now disciples the nation (and the rest of the world) in a God-denying secular philosophy. Eighty percent of media personalities don't believe in a personal God, heaven and hell, or fixed absolutes of morality.[11] They have helped blind the American conscience to the truth of God's Word and its application in everyday life.

I remember watching a major news anchor report on a devastating earthquake that hit Mexico City. He opened his story stating that in past times, people believed earthquakes were a mark of God's judgment. "Today," he said, "we know that earthquakes are only the shifting of the earth's plates."[12]

In other words, God and his judgments are old, and enlightened newscasters are in. What a sad removal of biblical truth from the realm of daily life.

Probably the greatest purveyor of deception in today's world is the seductive power of the music industry and its plethora of cassettes, CDs, and videos. From Elvis to Madonna, the message vibrates, "rebel, feel good, enjoy pleasure, and live for lust."

During the sixties and seventies, the Beatles led an entire generation of young people down the pathway of pleasure without God. With John Lennon proclaiming they were "more popular than Jesus Christ," they sang of sexual freedom (while living immorally), drug highs ("Lucy in the Sky with Diamonds"), and Eastern religions (George Harrison in "My Sweet Lord").

Worldwide, masses of young people danced to their beat and emulated their lifestyle. For the past three decades the hedonistic message has vibrated and expanded its mesmerizing reach. How many millions of consciences have been altered through the power of popular music?

Tactic Five: Destruction and Death

The final goal of the Satanic war is the destruction of as many lives as possible.

Each year over 1.5 million babies are grotesquely butchered in the aborturaries of the land. Abortion is big business with big bucks. Since 1973 we have systematically tithed to the devil over twenty-eight million human beings.[13] There has never been a larger global holocaust.

Child abuse now physically and psychologically maims some 2.6 million children annually. Most of it is done in the broken family home that little resembles the place of security and love that was once the pillar of the nation.[14]

Some friends of ours recently adopted three precious children under the age of five who were rescued from an abusive home. All had been sexually mistreated, poorly cared for, and generally neglected. The baby boy's head was severely flattened from being left unattended on his back for hours in a dirty crib. They were passive, emotionally dysfunctional, and developmentally damaged. After a year of tender care, they are beginning to laugh, play, and respond to love they should have received in their natural home.

Since 1960 the teen suicide rate has more than tripled. Suicide is now the third leading cause of death among adolescents.[15] Over 100,000 Americans have now died from AIDS—ninety-eight percent the result of promiscuous sexual behavior—and one million more carriers of the HIV virus will die in the next decade.[16]

A junior high honor roll student recently shocked our town by borrowing a gun and killing himself. Two weeks earlier, I'd spoken to a group of kids in our area on "Choosing Life," and nearly fifty percent stood and confessed having suicidal thoughts. After much weeping and prayer, many were delivered from an obsession with death. Two weeks later, their classmate ended his brief life—a sober warning of the need to walk in victory and truth.

America's violent crime rate is higher than any other industrialized nation. Eight out of ten Americans will be a victim of violent crime at least once in their lives.[17]

Euthanasia, the killing of the elderly or dying, is a rising trend. Dr. Jack Kevorkian, "Dr. Death," has succeeded in pointing the American people toward the acceptance of people ending their own lives.

American society is fast becoming a death culture with shootings, abortions, suicides, and violence filling the landscape with fear and despair. Much of this happened in your lifetime, before your very eyes.

Children At Risk

Picture your local school. Two generations ago it was a place of peace, security, and educational advancement. In 1940, its top ten problems were:

1. Truancy or tardiness
2. Running in the halls
3. Talking out of turn in class
4. Unfinished homework
5. Loitering after school
6. Unreturned library books
7. Chewing gum in class
8. Talking during study hall
9. Broken windows
10. Graffiti on walls[18]

Today, a flood of cultural decay has swept across the nation. No longer is school a safe and secure place. In the halls of Anywhere High, these are now the top ten problems:

1. Violence
2. Stealing
3. Forcible rape

4. Teacher abuse
5. Knives or guns
6. Vandalism
7. Destruction of property
8. Arson
9. Rebellion against authority
10. Gang warfare[19]

Quite a difference, isn't it? And it happened in such a short time. Kids were once safe at school, but now it's one of the most dangerous places to spend your time.

The neighborhood isn't safe either. Recently, the eyes of America anxiously watched the news of three ten- to eleven-year-old girls who were brutally murdered. Two were kidnapped in the Midwest, their bodies found in the woods some weeks later, mutilated and broken. A ten-year-old girl in California was kidnapped out of her own home during a slumber party. Her badly tortured body was found under garbage and bricks in a deserted alley.

This tragedy, and that of many others, is becoming commonplace in our land. A generation ago, such cruel murders were considered unthinkable. Today, they are simply bylines on the evening news. Our national conscience has gone mad.

Fifty years ago, we gasped when one swear word was uttered on the cinema screen. Today we hardly blink when a beautiful ten-year-old girl is cruelly and savagely murdered.

What has gone wrong in America? And who is really to blame?

Leading the Cultural Decay

Though many factors in our complex and diverse society have contributed to our breath-taking decay of national conscience, three primary influencers stand above the rest. Charles Finney's insightful words, revealing two of them, are worth a second look:

> Now what is the cause of this degeneracy? Doubtless there are many causes that contribute more or less directly to it, but I am persuaded that the fault is more in the *ministry and public press than in any and all things else.*[20]

Ministers and the public press. We would say today *pastors and the media.* The failure of these two leadership spheres are at the heart of our nation's decline.

Failure One: Pastors and Priests

In some ways, pastors and priests are to the Church what coaches are to athletic teams. Bad coaching, bad teams. If you have bad leadership, followers are left to flounder.

The most important leaders in the life of a nation are the ministers. If they faithfully live and teach the Word of God, then truth will bless the Church and the Church will brighten the world. If pastors fail, the Church and society become worldly.

In the Old Testament, God held the Jewish leaders responsible for the state of the nation. In Ezekiel 34:2b–10, God strongly warns the leaders of Israel that their lack of good leadership caused the disintegration of the people. Ezekiel declares:

" ' This is what the Almighty LORD says: How horrible will it be for the shepherds of Israel who have
been taking care of only themselves. Shouldn't
shepherds take care of the sheep? . . . You have not
strengthened those that were weak, healed those
that were sick, or bandaged those that were
injured. You have not brought back those who
strayed away or looked for those that were lost.
You have ruled them harshly and violently. . . . So,
you shepherds, listen to the word of the LORD:
This is what the Almighty LORD says: I am against
the shepherds. I will demand that they hand over
my sheep. . . .' "

Many times in Israel's past, the nation's spiritual leaders
became selfish, greedy, and unconcerned about the people—
causing the nation to slide into evil. Leaders lost their vision
of a Just and Holy God along with their compassion for those
they guided.

Spiritual leaders set the compass of a culture. If ministers
preach and live the truth and care for the true needs of their
people, the Body of Christ grows, matures, becomes strong,
and affects society around them.

One of my favorite examples is John Wesley, the founder
of Methodism. Through fifty years of tireless ministry, he
lived and proclaimed the power of the gospel in eighteenth-
century England. Over 100,000 people came to Christ, many
charities were founded, and his tracts and sermons helped end
the cruel child labor laws of his day and influence the abolition of slavery.

A secret of America's early success was the role of the pastors in society. Coming out of Pilgrim and Puritan traditions,

Christian ministers were highly respected as citizen leaders in colonial America.

Their authority came from their godliness. They not only taught the ways of God, but served as judges, civil magistrates, and dispensers of health, education and welfare. They were America's guardians of truth.

They preached on election days. They proclaimed God's standards during military conflicts. These ministers led the way in America's awakenings.

According to Joseph Tracy, the first historian of the Great Awakening, the humility and repentance of New England's pastors greatly fueled the revival of the 1700s. He said:

> Especially among pastors there was a sense of spiritual want; there was self examination; there was self-abasement and mourning for discovered want of fervor and constancy in God's service; there was prayer for pardon, and for grace to be faithful . . . a more teachable spirit.[21]

As ministers sought God and applied his truth to everyday life, churches were renewed, thousands converted, seminary enrollment doubled, and the nation was morally renewed.

There are over 300,000 ordained ministers in America today. Add Christian leaders and lay pastors and the number may rise to 500,000. That's about one pastor for every five hundred Americans.

The moral influence of these 500,000 men and women should be enormous. Instead, over the past forty years, the nation's moral and corporate conduct has nose-dived into immoral oblivion.

What happened?

First, many church leaders don't really know the God of the Bible nor believe in its truth. A recent study of mainline denominational ministers showed a major shift from biblical orthodoxy to a liberal view of Scripture. In the survey, fifty percent of those responding didn't believe in God as a Personal Being, seventy-five percent didn't believe in supernatural miracles, and forty-five percent didn't believe in heaven and hell as actual places.[22]

No wonder so many churchgoers are confused, hurting, and lost. The shepherds are lost themselves. A pastor friend once told me his seminary didn't have one born-again Christian either on staff or as a student. There were many "religious" people, but none exhibited the Christ-like character and integrity of God. Sadly, that is true of many ministers today.

Secondly, many Christian leaders have fallen into sin themselves. Adultery runs rampant. Stories of Jim Bakker's flagrant lifestyle and Jimmy Swaggart's meetings with prostitutes were the laughingstock of the press for years. Behind these visible figures were the moral failings of many other Christian leaders who gave in to the pressure of lust and power.

Thirdly, many good ministers have compromised the power of the gospel. Instead of leading Christians away from the idols of the world, we've closed the doors on Super Bowl Sunday and frequented the same movies that the secular world watches. Instead of transforming the culture, we've conformed ourselves to it.

In early '96, I spoke at a Revive America Seminar[23] in the Midwest that began on a Friday evening and lasted through Sunday. When I arrived, I learned that the concluding service on Sunday was scheduled at an odd time. The reason? It was Super Bowl Sunday. A number of pastors wanted to see the game at 5:00 P.M. and not offend their men.

God moved so powerfully during the service that many wept at the altar, some pastors stood and confessed the sin of making sports an idol, and few left the presence of God until the game was over. It didn't matter. Revival was more important than the world's best entertainment.

Not all Christian leaders have capitulated to the culture, but many have. That's why God's light grows dimmer in our nation. A recent *US News & World Report* poll confirmed that sixty-five percent of our people believe that religion is losing its influence on American life.[24]

Failure Two: the Media

Today's proliferation of media—including newspapers, magazines, radio, TV, the movie industry, music, video, and computer networking—dominates the American landscape. Everywhere you turn, radios are on, TVs run non-stop, and glitzy magazines wink from the newsstands. Endless information cascades at you like a mental Niagara Falls.

The media are not new. We've always possessed forms of communication. These are a gift from God that can be used either for good or evil. Yet, for the past few decades, the media have risen to control the development and flaunt the decadence of our culture in an unprecedented way. Why has this happened?

First, our spiritual leaders retreated. When the ministers stopped leading the people in understanding God's principles of justice and righteousness, the news commentators, movie

actors, and journalists stepped into the void. Someone needed to be heard and believed. Today's newsmakers became the
new priests of our world.

Secondly, the revolution in technology and birth of the
Information Age gave dazzling recognition to the new truth
peddlers. They were seen and heard twenty-four hours a day
in every household of the land. This increase in available
knowledge, at a time in which the influence of the Church
was waning, brought doom to the morals of the land.

Let's look briefly at the various tentacles of the media's
reshaping of America.

MUSIC

With the Church's retreat, a world-wide youth rebellion
exploded across the world from the 1960s to the present
greatly fueled by the rise of pop and rock music. Song is the
medium, and its words speak of defiance to parents, free love
and sex, lust of all kinds, anarchy, and unrestrained pleasure.

In the sixties, Elvis Presley, Jimi Hendrix, Janis Joplin,
Steppenwolf, the Grateful Dead, and the Rolling Stones were
but a few of the musical pied pipers whose songs molded the
values of the Baby Boom generation. We pointed out in chapter two that probably the most impacting group of that era
was the Beatles, whose songs first spoke of love and romance,
then progressed into open immorality, drug experimentation,
and Eastern mysticism. A whole generation followed them
into sexual sin, drug use, and pantheistic thought.

In the 1990s, groups such as Nirvana, Nine Inch Nails,
and the Butthole Surfers use grunge metal and gangsta rap
lyrics to encourage far more than individual hedonistic

pursuits—they openly promote lewd sex, violence and anarchy in many forms.

My home area was recently engulfed in controversy by a Butthole Surfers concert held at the county fairgrounds. Many churches, private citizens, and civic groups tried to stop the event due to the group's offensive and degrading name and the violent nature of some of their songs. One song's lyrics read: "She's been talkin' behind my back. She's gonna bleed when I kick her in the teeth."[25]

Even the hospital leadership warned in a letter to the editor of the safety hazards of allowing such a group to perform in the area. In the end, the county commissioners caved in to so-called First Amendment considerations and allowed the concert. That evening, Bremerton's Harrison Hospital saw a rash of injured teenagers who were physically hurt during the violence of the concert.

The philosopher George Santayana once said, "Let me write the ballads of a nation and I care not who makes its laws." Music is powerful. It drives the West's cultural values. Rock stars are idolized and imitated. MTV is the new living color bible. Bad music, in many forms, breaks down the inhibitions of human nature and plunges millions into broken relationships, venereal disease, hopelessness, and destructive behavior.

Baby boomers found out the hard way. Nineteen sixties rock 'n' roll glamorized free sex. Today ten million Americans have herpes,[26] one-half of all marriages ends in divorce,[27] and depression stalks the land.

NEWS JOURNALISM

A few years ago, the evening news anchor replaced the pastor as the weekly source of "truth" for most people. Every evening, seated in the authoritative desk, with videos and cut-outs of all the day's events, these bigger than life figures give us the "facts" about our world.

Unfortunately, they do more of the writing of the news than reporting it. Studies have shown that most of America's TV personalities do not believe in biblical values. The vast majority do not have a personal relationship with God. Eighty percent favor abortion and homosexuality. Most prefer a one world system of government over national sovereignty.[28]

Many of their messages are deceptive. I recently joined a friend on the set of a live TV news broadcast. The news anchor was a practicing homosexual who was obviously sympathetic to a gay rights story and very negative about an anti-abortion rally. I was saddened by the lack of truth he shared and sorry for the miserable bondage this man lived under.

The news media possess such power over our immoral and unthinking American culture that events can be framed to achieve their objectives. I personally believe that the election of Bill Clinton in 1992 as President of the United States was a clear example of pro-liberal media spin. Six months before the election, the media greatly distorted the state of the U.S. economy. George Bush was portrayed as a villain. Bill Clinton and Al Gore were cast by *Newsweek* magazine as the "Young Guns" who would set things straight. Many other newspapers and periodicals followed suit. In a matter of weeks, President Bush's ratings tumbled and Bill Clinton's soared. Only after the election did some major newspapers including the *Washington Post* and the *New York Times* admit the economic facts were greatly distorted.[29] By that time, it was too late.

Television and the Movie Industry

Probably the most pervasive authority in America today is the television set. The average American watches fifty hours of TV a week—ten hours more than the average work week.[30] While this preoccupation with entertainment is disturbing in itself, the greatest problem lies in the content of what people are watching.

There is more brutal violence and explicit sex on television than ever before—hence the need for V-chips in the new generation of sets. Marriage is ridiculed; immoral relationships are glamorized. The famous Murphy Brown flap, with Vice President Dan Quayle, is a perfect example of the media touting its values of immoral sex, single parenthood, and the no-need-for-fathers mentality.

By the time the average child reaches the age of eighteen, he will have witnessed more than fifteen thousand murders on the screen.[31] Research shows that extensive television watching makes it difficult for children to distinguish between fiction and reality. Certainly the increase in divorce, sexual sin, and exploding crime rate can be laid at the doorstep of television. Its passive dulling of the mind has assaulted every value that Americans once held dear. And though a 1991 survey showed that only two percent of respondents believed television should have the greatest influence on children's values, fifty-six percent believed that TV did have the greatest influence—more than parents, teachers, and religious leaders combined.[32]

Movie stars and the pictures they adorn are America's new heroes. Commanding multimillion dollar salaries, and kept before the public eye near every supermarket counter, today's starlets are clearly the gods and goddesses of the new world. We're glibly told of Madonna's hottest affair, Michael Jackson's latest payoff, and Liz Taylor's newest marriage breakup. Their quotes appear in newspapers and periodicals where spiritual leaders and moral statesmen once spoke.

Pulling out tonight's paper I read:

> Hugh Grant and Elizabeth Hurley made a grand entrance for "Extreme Measures," then remained extremely tight-lipped about the status of their relationship. "I refuse to talk to the press about my private life," Grant said, when he was asked if the couple's relationship has suffered from Grant's arrest with a Los Angeles prostitute."[33]

Are these "role models" and their foolish quotes the best we have to offer in America? Then why do we feature their pictures and remarks in our newspapers and magazines?

Almost everyone follows the movie stars to the theaters— including Christians. World Vision reports that Christians spend $6.60 of every $100 on entertainment, while they give only $1.20 to the Church for missions and ministries. The average teenager watches fifty R-rated movies a year.[34]

The combined influences of music, television, movies, video games, magazines, and newspapers have done untold damage to the American soul. Instead of leading us into the knowledge of God and his world, the media have encouraged us to forget about God and have a little fun. Only Judgment Day will reveal the true extent of the damage.

These two leadership spheres—Church leaders and media leaders—need our prayers. Not all of them have succumbed to the national moral avalanche, but most have been affected and intimidated by it. As you drive past the churches of your town or area, intercede fervently for their awakening. Encourage your own pastor and other spiritual mentors to lead the charge for reclaiming our decadent culture.

Years ago I began praying for a complete renewal of the American media. It is a lofty giant, but one that should submit to the dictates of conscience and principles of God's Word. Its return to sound moral perspectives would be a blessing to the entire world.

Though Christian leaders and the media are a key to reviving our national consciousness, there is a third group that really occupies the bottom line.

Failure Three: You and Me

The largest source of our nation's decline is found in *us*—you and I as individuals. We're all part of the moral rot of our world. We, too, have succumbed to the blindness of conscience threatening to destroy the very foundations of our once great society. We need to understand the part we've played.

The Freedom Train

For the next several chapters I'd like you to go on a little whistlestop tour through your own heart and mind.

I call it the Freedom Train. Using a series of helpful and honest questions, we want to weave our way through the attitudes and actions of our lives, looking at those areas where God wants to set us free. There are a number of important stops along the way. Jesus says in John 8:31–32:

> "If you live by what I say, you are truly my disci-
> ples. You will know the truth, and the truth will
> set you free."

Freedom comes by knowing the truth and living it—
with the help of a clear and sensitive conscience. On the other
hand, we are warned in the Bible that our conscience can
become dull or hardened through abuse or misuse—greatly
affecting our ability to be free. Paul says in 1 Timothy 4:1–2:

> The Spirit says clearly that in later times some believ-
> ers will desert the Christian faith. They will follow
> spirits that deceive, and they will believe the teach-
> ings of demons. These people will speak lies dis-
> guised as truth. Their consciences have been scarred
> as if branded by a red-hot iron.

In the same way that a burn kills nerve cells creating
numbness or lack of feeling, so our conscience can become
numb or dull through the "heat" of disobedience.

In the following section, we'll look at the symptoms or
marks of a dull conscience that can rob us of our freedom in
Christ. Most of the checkpoints on our Freedom Train tour
have come out of my own failures and experiences over the
course of a lifetime. It's been a wild, but liberating ride.

I encourage you to take your time in these chapters. Go
over each point carefully and honestly, allowing God to speak
to you, bringing understanding, change, and freedom to your
life. You may identify with many of the points—or maybe just
a few. Whatever the conviction, respond by faith to the voice
of the Holy Spirit. It's far better to go over this checklist now

than to face Judgment Day with a dull conscience, unprepared for God's loving scrutiny.

Healthy self-examination is a good starting point.

Paul said to the Corinthian believers, "Examine yourselves to see whether you are still in the Christian faith. Test yourselves!" (2 Corinthians 13:5).

With that exhortation in mind, let's let the journey to freedom begin.

FOR THOUGHT, DISCUSSION, AND ACTION

1. Why were American culture and morality relatively unchanged for 150 years? What happened during those years to maintain private and public virtue?

2. What changes in conduct and manners have you seen in your lifetime in this country? Which are you most concerned about? In which changes were you a part of the decline?

3. What are the five tactics of warfare that the enemy has used to destroy our social fabric? In what other ways has our national conscience weakened? Which one most concerns you?

4. What are the two greatest influencers in the decay of conscience in our nation? Which one is most important? Discuss these areas of influence and their impact on others.

5. Why are the Church and its leaders the conscience of a culture? What Scriptures teach this principle? What can you do

to encourage your pastors and other spiritual leaders to bring renewal to our cities and nations?

6. Which areas of the media have impacted your life negatively? Give examples. What positive forms of media have blessed your life and or geographical area?

7. Commit yourself to be an intercessor for pastors and other spiritual leaders. Begin this week to make a difference in your world. Never quit until righteousness is restored.

SECTION TWO

The Freedom Train

"I want to raise up a generation devoid of conscience." [1]   *—Adolph Hitler*

CHAPTER 3

Free to Serve God

THE FIRST DESTINATION on our Freedom Train journey relates to our relationship to God himself. Where do we stand before him? What is the state of our conscience toward our Creator, Savior, and Lord?

Before we answer that question, we need to remind ourselves that every sin we commit is ultimately disobedience to God that separates us from him and true freedom. Sin is a failure to remember that he is there and that his presence requires certain behavior of us.

The Bible is clear about the following facts:

- God hates sin (Psalm 7:11, Proverbs 8:13).

- Man's rebellion against God has hurt and grieved His heart (Genesis 6:5–6, Lamentations 1:16).

- We are accountable to him for everything we've done, including every careless word we've spoken (Romans 14:12, Matthew 12:36).

- No one will ultimately get away with any wrong behavior (Ecclesiastes 12:14, Romans 2:3).

- God requires growth in maturity and holiness in our lives (2 Corinthians 7:1, Hebrews 12:14).

- Jesus died for us to set us free from both the penalty and power of sin (Colossians 2:13–14, 1 John 3:9).

- Salvation includes the cleansing and renewing of our conscience (Hebrews 10:22, 1 Peter 3:21).

All dullness of conscience comes down to forgetting God. He is always with us. He sees everything we do. To forget God's presence and live our lives in disobedience to his commands is really a state of fantasy and bondage.

Much of the world lives in fantasy land and chains—oblivious to God. Yet, he's the greatest reality. It is a grave mistake to forget that he is there.

We should regularly examine our relationship to God. Are we consciously aware that he is watching everything we think, say, and do? Is our heart open to him? Do we understand that he loves us and wants only our good? Do we know that one day we will give an account to him for all of our actions?

One day in the future, all people will be examined by God—including believers. All that we've thought and done will be seen in complete detail. Those of faith, with good hearts and changed lives, will be ushered into his eternal kingdom. The unbelieving, who refused to repent of their selfishness and rebellion, will be separated from him forever.

Following are some stations of the mind we need to pull into and analyze our conscience toward God.

Stop One

Do I often neglect personal prayer and praise times? Do I often pray with little faith or passion? Does my mind regularly wander while I pray? Am I convicted enough to grow in my personal prayer life?

Spending time with God in prayer is a mark of our intimacy with him. If we know him, love him, and desire to see his kingdom grow on earth, we will make prayer a daily priority. Failure to pray is a sign that God is distant in our thoughts and in our lives. When we actively seek God's presence, conversation with him naturally flows.

Maybe you're like me. Sometimes I go to prayer and feel like a limp noodle. God seems gone, there is little burden or feeling, and my prayers rise about as high as the ceiling. Ever had that experience? Well, join the club. There's nothing unusual about it.

What's bad, though, is when we have these experiences as a result of dulling our consciences toward prayer. If our conscience is sensitive to God, instead of just walking away and forgetting it all—even during a season of testing or spiritual dryness—we'll cry out to him and ask him to help us grow and persevere.

Many of us treat God as a nonperson. We sit down to pray, and our mind wanders to last night's movie, today's shopping trip, or tomorrow's problem. Then after drifting awhile, we get up and leave the room without ever saying goodbye. If we treated our friends the way most of us treat God, we'd live in a lonely world!

Isn't it comforting that he understands? God knows we are human, and gives us much slack because of it. But, we do not want to abuse his graciousness by treating him like dirt. He should be our best friend. We should treat him as such during those times of quality conversation—the time we spend in prayer to him.

I'll never forget a prayer time I had one morning on the steps of the U.S. Capitol Building in Washington, D.C. Having recently faced some major leadership failures in my life, I stood alone and silent, pondering the future. Instead of praying I was worrying. Instead of trusting God I was wallowing in a large manure pile of self-pity over some of the mistakes I had made.

After enjoying the pity party for an hour, I asked God's forgiveness and began to pray, not fret. Immediately after getting my heart right, waves of God's love and cascading revelation came flowing through my being. He had good and wonderful plans for my future. The best was ahead!

While I'd been distant to God, he had been waiting to comfort and take me forward. All I needed was to humble myself and trust him. When I finally turned, he flooded my soul with peace.

And what about the importance of praise? If your conscience is awake to who God is, then praise will be the normal language of your heart and mouth. He is the most fabulous, incredible, unbelievable, fascinating Being in the Universe. Not only that, he died for your sins, loves you deeply, and wants to live inside you and be your friend forever. That's cause for celebration! We also need to think about his blessings more than we do.

A heart open to God will always show itself in the voice of praise and thanksgiving. God is so great! God is so good!

If you find yourself not thinking and feeling this way often, then your conscience has become extremely dull to who God really is. David, the man after God's own heart, put it this way:

> You make the path of life known to me. Complete joy is in your presence. Pleasures are by your side forever. (Psalm 16:11)

David also sang a lot. That's because he learned through a sensitive heart and mind to bask in the presence of God. We can learn too.

I have a friend who spends almost every evening strumming his guitar and cranking up his praise music on the back porch of his Colorado Rockies home. With a heart for worship, Fred enjoys the presence of God, oftentimes for hours. Being delivered from drugs, alcohol, and prison time gives him reason for exuberant praise. When Fred speaks, you know that he knows and is excited about God. Praise is the fuel of that fire.

Stop Two

When God shows me an area of right or wrong in my life, do I feel compelled to act immediately? Or is it too easy for me to procrastinate?

When God brings us true guilt or conviction, he wants us to deal with it now. God is wise and loving, and the release of his conviction comes to free us from selfishness and make us more like him.

He also possesses all knowledge, which includes perfect timing. God knows just the right moment to expose us to wrong and bring correction. After all, he knows us, our strengths and weaknesses, better than we know ourselves.

Ray Allen was a gifted writer, fundraiser, and organizer who nearly lost everything during the early eighties. After his wife left him and their two young children, he survived a cruel Texas winter in a cramped travel trailer in great despair and soul-searching. One day he heard the voice of God bringing loving correction to his heart over his pride and wrong priorities. He repented, asked God to forgive him, and began to lead a changed life.

Today Ray is a happily remarried and very successful Texas legislator who may soon become the speaker of the Texas House. "I learned to obey God in the school of brokenness," he tells his audiences. "God knew the right time and way to bring me to my knees. I stopped making excuses for my behavior and said 'Yes, Sir!' God honored that."[2]

Procrastination is a blindness to God's reality, a denial of his wisdom, or laziness. If you feel convicted about an area of wrong in your life, then you should act immediately. If God wanted you to work on it tomorrow or next year, then he would reveal it to you then. The fact that he has brought conviction right now is ample evidence that he wants you to change and obey now.

Some people have even squandered their opportunity for salvation by not obeying God when he spoke to them. The Scripture says, "... we urge you not to let God's kindness be wasted on you. . . . Listen, now is God's acceptable time! Now is the day of salvation!" (2 Corinthians 6:1–2).

How many millions of people have heard gospel messages, felt convicted to give their lives to Christ, then refused that conviction, and are lost today? They had their moments. God chose the best and right times. But with a seared conscience, they turned away, and the conviction vanished. For some, it never returned.

Vladimir Lenin, the father of the Russian Bolshevik Revolution, studied the Bible when he was young and appeared close to becoming a Christian. After the untimely death of a brother, he hardened his heart and plunged into the socialist movement. He never moved back toward God, but brought the curse of ruthless atheism to the entire Soviet Empire. Years before his premature death in 1924, he'd missed the opportune time to give his life to Christ.

Joy Dawson, an international Bible teacher with Youth With A Mission, says delayed obedience is disobedience. It's also a mark of a dull mind that through repetition has grown used to resisting God.

Develop the habit of instant obedience. When God speaks, our answer should always be, "Yes, Lord!" He knows what we need and when we need it. That includes conviction of sin and encouragement in right living.

Stop Three

Am I afraid to analyze my motives? Do I examine my heart regularly?

Many people live their lives on a spiritual roller coaster. They think a wrong thought toward someone (heading down the track), develop their bad thinking into some selfish reactions, and don't deal deeply with their sin. Over a period of time, they fall to the bottom of the track with a guilty conscience and a broken relationship. Then they become convicted, repent of their sin, make the relationship right, and begin heading up the other side of the roller coaster. Things are okay for a while.

But soon, the pattern repeats itself. They lose their temper, have lustful thoughts, say unkind words, and don't deal with it fully. Again they head down the track, adding to their unclean life and hurting their conscience. Days go by. At some point they reach bottom again, come to their senses, change, and start coming up the track again.

During my teenage years, I played a game in my lustful thought life. During the week I'd sneak a look at a skin magazine. Sometimes I would browse at a newsstand, fully knowing that gazing at bathing beauties was bad for my spiritual health. On Sunday, I silently confessed my sin at church and felt better. The next week, I'd take the same lustful detours again.

Roller coaster Christianity doesn't produce strength or maturity. We should grow steadily toward the holiness and righteousness of God. Every day, God wants us to "be conformed to the likeness of his Son" (Romans 8:29 NIV). He doesn't want our lives to feel like a spiritual yo–yo that's up one day and down the next.

The key to steady growth is keeping your heart pure on a regular basis by allowing God to analyze your thoughts and motives. He knows them all anyway. We're the ones that need to know!

Years ago, I developed the habit of getting down on my knees at bedtime to ask God to search my heart. Using Psalm 139:23–24 as a guide, I invited the Lord to show me any sin that I'd committed that day. As he showed me, I repented, asked his forgiveness, and prayed for grace to not offend again. Once my heart and conscience were clear, I finished my prayers and hopped into bed. It was great to end each day with a clear conscience toward God and men. This daily inventory of thoughts and actions greatly speeded up change and growth in my life.

Now I try to keep these short accounts with God on a momentary basis. That means giving him access to my heart and motivations at all times. In 1 Corinthians 4:3–5, Paul said it this way:

> . . . I don't even ask myself questions. I have a clear conscience, but that doesn't mean I have God's approval. It is the Lord who cross-examines me. . . . He will also bring to light what is hidden in the dark and reveal people's motives. Then each person will receive praise from God.

Christian maturity blossoms when we give God access to our hearts and steadily shorten the time between disobedience and repentance. Failure to do so usually means we don't want to know. Failure to know is failure to grow.

Stop Four

Am I satisfied with my outward behavior when my heart is not right?

Your spouse asks you to take out the garbage. You're sprawled out in your favorite lounge chair reading the paper after a stressful day. Teeth clenched and heart disgruntled over this invasion of your free time, you trudge into the kitchen, gather up the trash, and do your duty.

There—you've gone through the motions and everybody should be happy, right? Wrong. There is something you've forgotten: "Humans look at outward appearances, but the LORD looks into the heart" (1 Samuel 16:7b).

God is never pleased with our actions if they do not come from right motivations. If your heart is not right, then the behavior is just "acting." This is what God likes:

> You are not happy with any sacrifice. Otherwise, I would offer one to you. You are not pleased with burnt offerings. The sacrifice pleasing to God is a broken spirit. O God, you do not despise a broken and sorrowful heart. (Psalm 51:16–17)

True, it's better to do the outward action than to do nothing at all. If you perform a wrong action with a bad heart, then two sins were committed. But to satisfy yourself with the outward action just to please people, is fakery and hypocrisy. God isn't fooled by it for a moment, and you shouldn't be either.

A person who learns to do the right things when the heart is not in it lives in an illusion. With a numb conscience toward God, his life becomes a masquerade of virtuous performance. Don't lie to yourself. That can be awfully dangerous to your spiritual life.

Stop Five

Do I put off the discussion of important things and talk about lighter topics with no feelings of conviction?

It was the Sunday night evangelistic service at Valley Road Baptist Church in Auckland, New Zealand. Geoff

Davies, a neighbor friend of mine who attended church but wasn't a professing believer, was seated next to me. The visiting evangelist was delivering a powerful and convicting message.

At the end of the service, the evangelist invited people to come forward to get right with God. Geoff's palms were sweaty, and his feet were tapping nervously on the floor. It was easy to see that he knew he should go forward. The conviction that God was speaking to him was written all over his face. I was praying silently, but Geoff didn't move.

The service ended and Geoff walked guiltily into the foyer. Seeing a friend from work, he blurted, "Hey, did you catch the football game last night? Real nail-biter . . ."

As I gazed after them, Geoff and his friend struck up a conversation and walked outside. After a few minutes, Friday night's game was all that occupied their minds.

The moment of conviction was gone. Very possibly, so was Geoff's salvation—if he continued to harden his heart and not respond to God. To this day, Geoff is an unregenerate man.

Whenever God speaks to us about something, we must never change the channel. If God is speaking to us, he has something important to say. To switch gears and talk about something lighter is not only rude, it can lead to great spiritual loss.

I remember another time of sharing Christ with a man in Argentina. As I laid out the gospel and helped him see his need for Jesus, conviction formed all over his face. The Holy Spirit was really zeroing in on him.

As I prepared to draw in the net, suddenly, almost out of nowhere, his face changed, he looked me in the eye, and casually remarked, "Well, how do you like our country? You like the weather, the food . . ."

In a few moments, the reality of important eternal things was completely lost in trivia. Sadly, we parted without the man experiencing the joy of a changed heart and without his name being written in the book of life.

Postponing the discussion of important things to talk about those of lesser value is a mark of a seared conscience. It's a method of running from God.

Stop Six

Do I feel convicted every time I'm selfish?

Every act of sin hardens and numbs our conscience. The more we do it, the more seared we become in that area of our lives.

God originally designed us to feel great remorse over all acts of rebellion. When Adam and Eve ate the forbidden fruit, feelings of guilt rushed upon hearts that previously hadn't experienced the pains of conscience. Hiding among the bushes, they showed great fear and remorse over what they'd done. Their consciences were awake, but they'd never be so sensitive again.

If you find that you can sin in certain areas and not feel convicted about it, then you've allowed your conscience to become dull. You've probably sinned so often in this category you are no longer sensitive. This is a dangerous place for the heart and mind to be.

Your conscience is your mental security alarm. Sirens go off in your mind because there is cause for alarm. You're about to disobey God.

Jessica knew she shouldn't be having sex with Ryan. She'd been raised in church, and knew that immorality was wrong. Now she was single, in her twenties, and in need of some love and attention. After dating Ryan for a few weeks, she resisted that little voice inside and gave in to his lustful desires and her own insecurities.

God soon became a distant memory. She also became lonelier, infected with herpes, and further down the road to a Christless eternity.

Nothing is more serious than disobeying God. The consequences are many. That's why the Bible encourages us to ". . . cleanse ourselves from everything that contaminates body and spirit and live a holy life in the fear of God" (2 Corinthians 7:1).

There are many other ways that a dull conscience shows itself in relationship to God. People with bad consciences:

- deny God's work in their lives
- ignore his warnings
- rationalize his existence
- forget him completely
- take his name carelessly in vain
- blast his reputation
- ridicule his Church
- hate his loving conviction
- laugh at his standards
- neglect his presence

. . . and commit many other types of sin.

All of these things we do to our own temporal and eternal loss. We also break and grieve God's heart.

Who's Really The Boss?

A person with a dull mind toward God is unwilling to let his Creator be the boss of his life. He's not free to serve God. Self and sin are more important to him than God's honor and glory.

Jesus came to get us off the fence and commit ourselves to God. He revealed God's love for us, died in our place, and now empowers us through the Holy Spirit to live a new life.

These first stops on the Freedom Train tour should point us toward committed faith in the God who is always with us. The closer we are to him, the more free we will be.

He wants your whole heart. Meditate on these important words:

> Love the LORD your God with all your heart, with all your soul, and with all your strength. (Deuteronomy 6:5)

> The LORD's eyes scan the whole world to find those whose hearts are committed to him and to strengthen them . . . (2 Chronicles 16:9)

> . . . we must get rid of everything that slows us down, especially the sin that distracts us. We must run the race that lies ahead of us and never give up. We must focus on Jesus, the source and goal of our faith . . . (Hebrews 12:1–2)

Are your eyes fixed on Jesus, or do you more easily focus on yourself? If so, you need to refocus your vision in his direction—to know and adore the God in whom "we live and move and exist" (Acts 17:28 NASB).

Start today to open your heart to him. Use this brief stop on our journey to freedom as healthy preparation for Judgment Day. In eternity, we'll painfully see the riches we've missed in distancing ourselves from him. If we open our hearts today, those riches can be ours.

FOR THOUGHT, DISCUSSION, AND ACTION

1. Why is a dull conscience toward God the height of fantasy? Is there anything more important than a sensitive heart to God? Why or why not?

2. Do you treat God as your best friend? Compare your relationship to him with that of a close friend. What can you do to draw closer to him?

3. Name the six areas of seared conscience in relationship to God. Which one are you most guilty of? What others can you think of? Discuss.

4. Be aware of God's presence. Learn to hear and obey his voice. Encourage others to be sensitive to him in all areas of their lives.

CHAPTER 4

Free to Love Yourself

IT'S HARD TO believe that our self-centered world has a seared conscience about the way we treat ourselves. Looking out for Number One is the spirit of the age. Stores sell countless self-improvement books. The advertising world figured out a long time ago that to sell products you must answer the question, "What's in it for me?"

Self-absorption is at the center of our moral decay. It's the heart of the problem.

Yet, not all self-focus is wrong. God wants us to love ourselves—but only in balance with loving him the most and our fellow human beings equally.

A lawyer once asked Jesus, "Teacher, which commandment is the greatest in Moses' Teachings?"

He was probably just asking about priorities—about what to live for. Jesus answered, " 'Love the Lord your God with all your heart, with all your soul, and with all your mind. . . . Love your neighbor as you love yourself' " (Matthew 22:37–39).

This chapter will look at loving ourselves, not in isolation or selfish exaltation, but the way God intended.

We are to love our neighbor as we love ourself. That means being a good steward of the one very special life God gave you.

As I pointed out in my book *If God Has A Plan For My Life, Why Can't I Find It?*, each of us has a unique destiny. When we die to selfish ambition and ask God to show us his plans for our lives, he can lead each of us to become the person we were born to be. That's true fulfillment. It's being a good steward of your closest possession—your own spirit, soul, and body.

Bruce Olson, the famous missionary to the stone age Molitone tribe in Venezuela, nearly missed God's call on his life by becoming a professor of languages at a well-known university. One evening at a church missions conference, God spoke to his heart about becoming a missionary.

"But why are you making me a missionary?" Bruce asked in his mind. "Why can't I serve you here in Minneapolis?"

His aim was to become a professor of languages and to get a Ph.D. in philology. But something within him said, "That isn't what God wants you to do."

"God, missionaries are ridiculous," he argued. "They wear tennis shoes in the pulpit. Their prayer letters aren't even written in decent English. They're failures, Lord. They can't make it in normal life, so they go off to be missionaries.

"But I can succeed here, Father. Everyone agrees. Why should I have to work with naked, starving people?"

God never told him why. But he did change Bruce's heart. Gradually his pleasant sane dream about becoming a linguistics professor vanished into this ridiculous idea of going to other countries to talk to savages about God. God didn't force him. But Bruce found himself irresistibly interested in other countries, in other cultures. As he continued to read, South America captured his attention, and he began to identify with the people there. Soon he found himself dreaming of this enchanting land and her people. He gave in to God. Bruce told a friend that he'd been "called" to be a missionary to South America.[1]

The rest is history. By following God's plan for his life, Bruce Olson reached an entire tribe for Christ and became one of the great missionaries of the twentieth century. But it took a holy commitment to God's will.

God's requirement for your life is holiness. "But because the God who called you is holy you must be holy in every aspect of your life. Scripture says, 'Be holy because I am holy' " (1 Peter 1:15–16). Holiness is being set apart for his purposes. It's being the person he created and saved you to be.

Self-fulfillment comes when you live God's plan for your life. That's the opposite of living for self. It's living for God and keeping a pure conscience that helps you take good care of your life.

This is an important segment of the Freedom Train ride. Many of us need to rekindle the fire of God's blueprint for our lives, producing true freedom and joy. What are some symptoms of a dull conscience toward loving ourselves?

Stop One

Am I careless with my health? Do I take care of my body as God would want me to?

Paul said to the carnal Corinthians who specialized in some dull areas of conscience:

> Don't you know that your body is a temple that belongs to the Holy Spirit? The Holy Spirit, whom you received from God, lives in you. You don't belong to yourselves. You were bought for a price. So bring glory to God in the way you use your body. (1 Corinthians 6:19–20)

God wants us to take care of ourselves. He wants us to be useful and fruitful by being a good steward of our physical body. This applies in many different areas.

BEING OVERWEIGHT

I put on some extra pounds during the years we lived in Washington, D.C. It must have been the good restaurants and pork barrel lunches with politicians. Soon my lower body looked more like Baby Huey than Arnold Schwarzenegger. Under conviction, I began to jog. It was painful, but I knew God wanted me to get back in shape. Slowly but surely, I made my way back to that thirty-four-inch waistline.

Now that we live in Washington state, I still struggle to pull myself out of bed to take a morning run. Sometimes it's pitch black and pouring cats and dogs. It rains a lot in the Pacific Northwest. Rumor has it that when Jesus returns, he'll be coming to our area. The Bible says he'll be coming with the *clouds* and will *rain* forever.

As I huff and puff, with aching muscles and sore joints, dodging dogs and cars, I remind myself of my past failure. God wants me to care for my body. He doesn't want me to worship exercise, rather just be as healthy as I can for him. I feel better and serve him with increased stamina when I'm not overweight. Watching my weight is loving myself.

LACK OF SLEEP

I recently read an article that said that seventy percent of Americans are sleep deprived. This leads to billions of dollars in lost production and much family- and work-related stress. The article pointed out that before the invention of electricity, people used to sleep on average ten to eleven hours a night. Wouldn't that be great! Most of us try to get by on five or six. That hurts our bodies, our minds, and our effectiveness for God.

A lawyer friend of mine named Ken Smith convinced me a few years ago to get enough sleep. His daily habit was to go to bed at eight o'clock and rise at four every day. Getting those eight hours of sleep gave him the edge to handle his responsibilities.

Though I couldn't go to bed at eight, I tried it. What a difference it has made. It's not easy to do because we have six children, a busy household, and all the twentieth century temptations. But Ken's principled lifestyle is a constant example to me. If you're not getting enough sleep, then your body and life are probably suffering for it.

Do yourself a favor. Stay in bed longer—even if it takes gut wrenching discipline.

POOR DIET

Studies now show that at least fifty percent of American health problems today are behavior related—usually due to an extremely poor diet. Our empty-calorie, high-fat, high-sugar fast food diet is hurting most Americans. Today there are fast food restaurants everywhere and mini-marts at many gas stations. Readily available junk food makes it harder to be good to our bodies. Add to this the presence of chemicals, caffeine, and other poisons, and you have an entire society with a poorer quality of life despite the wonders of modern medicine. We're shooting ourselves in the foot with bad eating habits.

CLEANLINESS

It's not true that "cleanliness is next to godliness," but unless there are extenuating circumstances that prohibit it, cleanliness is a mark of good stewardship. As they say in the inner city, "God don't make no junk." He also doesn't want us to junk our lives, cars, homes, or anything else we possess. Orderliness, including keeping ourselves and possessions in good shape, is a sign of God's character within us.

Several times I've stayed in homes heaped to the ceiling with clutter and rubble. They were sorry places to visit, let alone to live in. If God can change our hearts, then he can certainly help us to clean up our kitchens. Self-control inside of us should produce orderliness on the outside. If it doesn't, then we know our conscience needs sharpening.

DRUGS AND ALCOHOL

One of the saddest expressions today of the lack of self-love is the drug and alcohol epidemic. People get involved with drugs and drink for many different reasons, but never with a clear conscience. They simply destroy their lives through the consumption of poisons. How carelessly and casually we accept it. What glaring evidence this is of a darkened heart and mind that is not loving itself.

Danny Lehmann was a teenage surfer in California who spent years of his life riding waves, partying, and getting high.

Regular drug use was starting to wither his body and erode his mind. One day, while totally stoned at the beach in Santa Cruz, Danny was handed a Christian tract. Groggily, he waded through God's plan for freedom from sin. Within twenty-four hours, he surrendered his life to Jesus and began renewing his mind in God's word. With the help of a renewed conscience, he is now one of Youth With A Misson's most successful evangelists.

God wants you to take care of your body. This applies to many other areas of your physical life. Awaken your conscience and really love yourself! It'll be a blessing to you—and to God and others.

Stop Two

Am I careless with my time? Do I sometimes influence others to use their time unwisely?

Time is one of the most precious things we possess. Our busy world has caused time to become the currency of the age—greater in its importance than money. Yet how few use their time to glorify God and truly benefit self and others. Our consciences are dull, especially to the reality of eternity.

When I was a child, I heard this little saying:

> *One small life shall soon be past.*
> *Only what's done for Christ will last.*

It took many years for me to really come to grips with this idea. Like most teenagers and young adults, I felt that I possessed all the time in the world. Now, as I get older, I realize how precious time is.

You and I have one life to live. Especially from God's viewpoint our life is extremely short. We must handle it carefully with much prayer. As Moses cried out, we need God's help to "number each of our days" (Psalm 90:12).

Beyond this life is eternity. Only our relationship with Christ and the people we touch for him will remain to see the next world. That one lasts forever.

How important it is to use our time for God and his kingdom. Doing this daily changes our lives and priorities. Outside our routine survival responsibilities, we should wisely use each second we have for lasting eternal purposes. The Bible calls this "redeeming the time" (Ephesians 5:16 KJV). Only a dull conscience causes us to waste our lives on trivial pursuits.

And influencing others to waste their precious time is like robbery. Nothing else a man possesses is as nonrenewable as his time. Yet we sometimes carelessly shoot the breeze with friends, encourage a co-worker to slough off on the job through our bad example, or invite others to endless activities that have no value in eternity.

While in college, God really convicted me of being a time waster. Instead of using this important time to prepare for life, I hung out, tossed Frisbees, and goofed around in my free time. So did most of my friends. That seemed to be what university life was all about.

On Judgment Day our consciences will be extremely sensitive in God's presence. For many, this will be a terrifying moment of regret as we gaze on the landscape of our lives, littered with missed opportunities and empty pursuits.

It doesn't have to be. Ask God to revive your conscience now, and live the rest of your days as a steward of your time.

Stop Three

Do I struggle against personal discipline for the sake of my own convenience without feeling bad about it?

God bestows a gift on those that follow him, "... a spirit of power, of love, and of self-discipline" (2 Timothy 1:7 NIV). If that verse is true, then he has precious few followers who have opened the package!

A breakdown of discipline characterizes our time. Even the word seems harsh and culturally out of vogue. Scripturally, discipline is a key to a successful life. Paul told Timothy:

> Discipline yourself for the purpose of godliness; for bodily discipline is only of little profit, but godliness is profitable for all things, since it holds promise for the present life and also the life to come.
> (1 Timothy 4:7–8 NASB)

After all, the word *disciple* comes from the word *discipline*. Disciples of Jesus are disciplined followers of his. How foreign this sounds to our easygoing lingo. Can't you just hear it: "Hey, a believer's a believer. Don't throw on me this heavy discipline stuff. That's legalism from the dark ages."

No, discipline is a mark of a follower of Jesus. Without discipline God can't use our lives effectively. Nor can we be wise stewards of our time. Unless we're disciplined, we won't keep our temples in good shape for the Master.

The organization I serve with—Youth With A Mission—was started by Loren and Darlene Cunningham in 1960 through tireless effort and exhaustive personal discipline. Loren still travels to scores of nations each year, spreading the gospel message and training indigenous leaders. He has personally ministered in every nation on earth. His effective and well-used life is a living testimony of the character qualities of discipline, hard work, and the sacrificial pursuit of a God-given vision. Eating right, sleeping wisely, and staying in shape have all contributed to the goal.

It's a small wonder that the devil wants us to be negative about discipline. Without it, we can't do much of anything for the Lord.

Sometimes we even joke about our lack of self-control. "I'm so undisciplined," we giggle as we help ourselves to more dessert. I don't think God laughs at the lack of discipline in the Church and world as a whole. I believe he weeps over the body we will waste, time we'll squander, and victories we won't win.

God is looking for a generation that will awaken their hearts and open God's gift of self-discipline. Why don't you be one of them? More discipline will bless you and help you be a blessing to others.

Stop Four

Do I have little conscience regarding what I wear? Do I dress for current fashions or comfort instead of to glorify God?

This is a controversial one. Please don't pick up your baseball bat until you've heard me out. A certain deadening of conscience in the area of dress has greatly numbed the Western world. Its effects get worse everyday. The heart of it is not the matter of dress—but it shows itself symptomatically in the clothes we wear or don't wear.

One generation ago, someone came up with a novel idea that men and women really weren't that different—not a new idea—it just hadn't been popular for centuries. They said we were all the same and should dress alike, wear our hair alike, and blur into one.

They called this idea unisexualism—the oneness of the sexes. So men let their hair grow, clothing styles began to change, and men and women—especially young people—began to look alike.

I remember my Grandma Boehme asking me on a number of occasions when we were out in public together during the sixties and seventies, "Is that a boy and girl, two girls, or two boys?" I didn't know. Their grooming and dress were the same.

This cultural shift to a unisexual standard was done in the name of freedom and equality. But was that the heart of it? I don't think so. I believe it was a tactic of the devil to destroy both the self-worth and complimentary functions of men and women. Another goal was to destroy the family unit.

The Bible teaches clearly that men and women are equal in value (Genesis 1:27, 1 Peter 3:7), but unequal in role and function (Ephesians 5:22-33, 1 Peter 3:1-7, and numerous other texts). One reason for these created differences may be to demonstrate different aspects of the character of God. Men display the masculine traits (physical strength, rationality, and family authority) with roles that go along with them. Women demonstrate the feminine characteristics (physical beauty, intuition and emotion, and family nurture) that produce a complementary role within marriage.

These differences in the two sexes are healthy and beneficial. They're a part of God's design. When men fulfill their role in family and society, their self-esteem soars and family life is stable. When women perform their God-given responsibilities, feminine self-worth blossoms and blesses the culture. As David Wells points out in his insightful book *No Place for Truth,* it was the stability of Christian womanhood in early America that gave the culture its backbone and continuity.

The complementary roles of men and women have historically shown themselves in the distinction between men and women's clothing. Look carefully at God's principle of sexual difference in Deuteronomy 22:5:

> A woman must never wear anything men would wear, and a man must never wear women's clothes. Whoever does this is disgusting to the LORD your God.

Pretty strong words. Another translation says that mixing men and women's clothing standards is "an abomination to the Lord your God" (NASB). It's a thing that God hates.

But wait a minute. Don't the pictures you've seen of the Old Testament show everybody wearing robes? They all dressed the same—or at least that's how the artists drew them.

Obviously, that wasn't true. If God's words in Deuteronomy 22:5 mean anything, males and females dressed very differently in olden times—even if they both worked out in the fields. God hated anyone who blurred those distinctions.

The New Testament teaches this principle. Paul told women to "dress modestly with decency and propriety, not with braided hair or gold or pearls or expensive clothes, but with good deeds, appropriate for women who profess to worship God" (1 Timothy 2:9–10 NIV). Here Paul brings in the importance of modesty and decency in our clothing motivations.

Clothing differs from culture to culture, but maleness and femaleness doesn't. With God's Word as our compass, we should seek to create a distinction between the way men dress (with the characteristics of masculinity in mind) and the way women dress (highlighting the unique qualities of femininity).

Thirty years into the unisex revolution, this concept seems archaic and foreign. But which is biblical: what we practice today or what the Bible teaches?

America lived these principles for almost two hundred years. Men wore masculine-type clothing and women wore feminine attire. That's a simple historical fact. Women were cherished and protected as the weaker of the two sexes (1 Peter 3:7), and men fulfilled their masculine responsibilities. The results were healthy families and boys and girls with good self-esteem.

When I was a junior in high school, the unisexual movement that had been underway for some time invaded our town. The dress code went first. Increased immorality and confusion of sex roles followed. Twenty years later this movement to destroy God-designed maleness and femaleness has given us:

- women joining military combat units and men wearing jewelry.
- blatant nudity and sensuality.
- transsexualism and gross perversion.
- militant homosexuality and lesbianism. Sodomy, the biblical term, is the natural result of fuzzy sexual

understanding. Men no longer understand masculinity; women are confused about godly femininity.

- date rape and sexual abuse where women and children are not protected.
- total family breakdown and millions of sons and daughters with low self-esteem.

Now, I'm not attributing these problems solely to the change in clothing. Yet we need to see the ramifications of our seared consciences regarding male and femaleness that's shown itself in what we wear.

In our current dress standards, we've stepped on history and the Bible, followed the flow, and hardened our hearts and minds. We dress the way we want, for comfort and convenience; or by what's in stores and fashion magazines. We are a part of the problem, not the solution. Blurred sexual roles are glaring evidence of a dying civilization that has turned its back on the principles of God's Word—even in the area of dress.

I believe that many of us need to pray over our closets. If we'd done that twenty years ago, we wouldn't be in as great a moral fog as we presently find ourselves. We need to practice this Scripture in many gray areas of our lives:

> So, whether you eat or drink, or whatever you do,
> do everything to the glory of God. (1 Corinthians 10:31)

Whatever you do. That doesn't leave out anything, does it? It must include dress.

On a trip to Texas, a friend of mine was disappointed not to see cowboys on the streets. She finally met a tall, athletic seventy-year-old man in jeans, boots, and a dapper cowboy hat. She explained why she was thrilled to meet at least one cowboy.

In a strong southern drawl he explained why he dressed western: "Long about 1970, men's fashions became just too darlin' for me. I walked into a western shop where clothes looked like men's. I've been dressing this way ever since."

Do I Really Love Myself?

There are many other ways that we can have dull hearts toward ourselves. Actually, any neglect of self in body, soul, or spirit devalues the precious treasure God has given to us. That treasure is you, and he wants you to treat yourself accordingly. While putting him first, and caring for others equally, he longs for us to be free to cherish our own gift of life.

This important stop on the Freedom Train contains a checklist of the stewardship of our destiny. God wants you to be set apart for the work of his kingdom. A holy conscience will guarantee a holy and productive life. Please meditate on these verses:

> May the God who gives peace make you holy in every way. May he keep your whole being—spirit, soul, and body—blameless when our Lord Jesus Christ comes. (1 Thessalonians 5:23)

> Therefore, your minds must be clear and ready for action. . . . Because you are children who obey God, don't live the kind of lives you once lived.

> Once you lived to satisfy your desires because you didn't know any better. But because the God who called you is holy you must be holy in every aspect of your life. (1 Peter 1:13–15)

> We also pray that the Lord will greatly increase your love for each other and for everyone else, . . . Then he will strengthen you to be holy. Then you will be blameless in the presence of our God and Father when our Lord Jesus comes with all God's holy people. (1 Thessalonians 3:12–13)

Have you allowed your conscience to become dull toward self? Do you feel like the steward of the life God has given you?

Start today to love yourself with a holy conscience guiding the way. God has much for you to do. You have one life to live. Live it to the fullest in freedom and blessing to the glory of God.

FOR THOUGHT, DISCUSSION, AND ACTION

1. What's the difference between being selfish and loving yourself? Define each. Why does God want us to love ourselves as we do our neighbor?

2. Look up the word stewardship. What does it mean to be a good steward of yourself? In what areas of personal stewardship are you weak? In what areas are you strong? Discuss.

3. How do you practice the principle: "Whatever you do, do all to the glory of God?" How does this apply to your health, time, appearance, personal disciplines? What have been the effects of unisexualism in our world?

4. Pray over your closet and dress to glorify your Creator. Eat right. Sleep well. Enjoy the freedom that a good conscience brings to your personal life.

CHAPTER 5

Free to Do Right

GOD ASKED JONAH to travel to the most evil city of his time—Nineveh. For us, would that be like going to New York? Paris? Baghdad? The people in Nineveh hated God and worshipped idols. Jonah thought their consciences were dead.

So he took a detour through a big fish. After learning it didn't pay to disobey his own conscience, he made it to Nineveh and began to preach.

To his shock and anger, the Ninevites listened to his message and changed their ways. But their turnaround made Jonah look bad. He'd said they'd be destroyed in forty days, and now because of their repentance and God's forgiveness, he looked like a false prophet.

So, at the end of the book of Jonah we find the sulking prophet sitting under a plant outside the city. First it shades him, and he's happy. Then it shrivels and dies, and he gets mad. Then God speaks to Jonah:

> "Do you think it's right for you to be angry because of the plant?"

"It is right for me to be angry! I will stay angry until I die!" answered Jonah.

And the Lord said, "You showed concern for the plant. But you did not plant it or make it grow. It appeared in the night and the next day it died. Then surely I can show concern for the great city Nineveh. There are many animals in that city. And there are more than 120,000 people living there. those people simply don't know right from wrong!" (Jonah 4:9–11, New Century Version)

Times don't really change; we've just added some people and some technology. Today's world is much like Nineveh's. People simply don't know right from wrong. We used to know. However, in one generation our hearts have become so dull that few mention the "M" word, *morality,* as being relevant. A good conscience is sensitive toward right and wrong. Choosing to do right in all areas of life is crucial to having and maintaining a clear conscience.

In this chapter, we will stop at a number of checkpoints relating to personal morality. Prior to Jonah's preaching, the Ninevites were blind to personal areas of right and wrong. In one of the most sudden reversals of history, they changed and received forgiveness and blessing from God.

Where do you stand on morality? Are you sensitive toward right and wrong in all areas of your life? Here are some important stops on the journey to freedom in personal morals.

Stop One

Am I sometimes apathetic about right and wrong?

God cares passionately about right and wrong. He loves right and hates wrong (Hebrews 1:9). He revealed these standards of behavior first through the Law, then through his Son, and finally included them in the Bible.

For nearly two thousand years, the Bible has been the Western world's clearest compass for right and wrong behavior. It has brought untold blessing to people and nations who've obeyed its principles. It also accurately describes the grief that comes when men reject God's ways for living.

We live in a time of biblical disobedience. We might as well be back in Nineveh. People have rejected God and his Word, they've rejected right and wrong, and we're suffering as a result.

Whenever you find yourself being apathetic regarding right and wrong, you can know that your conscience is blackened. Apathy is moral numbness. An awakened heart is very sensitive toward sin. It will deeply desire doing the right thing, and detest what is wrong. It has a passion for righteousness.

During my teenage years, before I committed my life to Christ, I allowed my conscience to become dead and dry toward right and wrong. I developed a foul mouth. I began to look at skin magazines and books. A creeping darkness began to envelop my heart and mind. Lust, profanity, sarcasm, and boredom were daily companions.

If you'd asked me during that time if I were doing what's right, I'd probably have responded, "Who cares? Who knows what's right or wrong anyway."

Pretty stupid answer. God knows. He always has. So do all the angels. So do godly people who are committed to his Word. Because of a love of right and hatred of wrong, there is total sensitivity to morality. Doing what's right is a consuming priority.

I'll never forget sharing the gospel with a guy and his girlfriend in Scotland. We were in a park in Edinburgh where we met, struck up a conversation, and got deeply involved in a discussion of right and wrong. The girl was from a Christian family and knew the Bible. When she'd first met her boyfriend, she knew it was not right for her to have sex with him. Her conscience was very sensitive to that truth. After disobeying and getting involved with him, her conscience bothered her. Now, a few years later, her conscience was burdened and guilty, but dull enough to tolerate the sin.

After talking with her for a while, she finally blurted out in anger and with some confused conviction, "Who knows what's right or wrong anymore? I don't really care!"

She'd turned one hundred and eighty degrees from her childhood faith and understanding of morality.

Who knows what's right or wrong? God did, and so did she. She didn't care anymore—but God did. So should we.

A confused sense of right and wrong pulls you into a pit of sin, guilt and confusion. It will eventually lead you to a place called hell.

We are all like that girl when we allow sin to dull our sensitivity to right and wrong. It doesn't matter what the area of morality is. If it's right, we need to embrace it, and if it's wrong we need to run from it. Paul said to Timothy:

> Stay away from lusts which tempt young people.
> Pursue what has God's approval. Pursue faith,
> love, and peace together with those who worship
> the Lord with a pure heart. (2 Timothy 2:22)

Stop Two

Do I treat all of my actions as right or wrong?

Many of us have a funny concept of right and wrong. Depending on our knowledge of the Bible, we know some things are "right" for us to do. These are our Do's. They might include loving God, loving people, praying, reading our Bibles, sharing our faith, going to church etc.

We also know some things that are "wrong" to do. These are our DON'TS. This list might include swearing, lying, cheating, fornicating, being greedy, *et cetera*. We can show these on a graph as follows:

A WRONG CONCEPT OF MORALITY

Moral	*Amoral*	*Immoral*
Do's	**Doesn't Matter**	**DON'TS**
Love God	Television	Swear
Love people	Hobbies	Lie
Pray	Recreation	Greed
Read Bible	Music	Murder
Evangelize	Dress	Lust

Did you notice the area in the center of the graph? Some of us don't consider these areas of our lives as right or wrong. They might include movies, sports, friends, reading material, etc.

Many of us live our lives with this huge middle area of gray. We've defined right and painted it white, then painted black the things we know are wrong. But much of our lives are lived in a very dull shade of gray. In these areas, we don't think so much about right and wrong. Sometimes it even changes from circumstance to circumstance.

But this compartmentalized understanding of morality is not God's idea. Here's a truer perspective: *everything you do is either right or wrong, depending on your motive or faith.*

That's right. *Everything.* There is no gray in God's eyes. It's true that consciences differ on many subjects where God's Word allows freedom and diversity of expression. But the Bible also teaches very clearly that in these relative areas, "Anything that is not done in faith is sin" (Romans 14:23).

Doubtful actions in those hazy areas of life are sinful. Everything we do should be done with our best "light" or faith. We should always be asking what's right or best. This is faith in action.

In other words, we need to consider the rightness or wrongness of every situation:

- Is it right or wrong to be watching this movie?
- Is it right or wrong for me to use my time by going to this sports event?
- Is it right or wrong to dress this way?
- Is it right or wrong to be involved in this hobby or be doing it at this time?

A saintly old man named Nate had a sign on his television that said, "Would Jesus watch this show with me?" That's living faith in questionable areas.

This is really the idea of Lordship in operation. As Lord, Jesus is the Boss of every area of our lives. There aren't just a few Dos and DON'Ts. We are to place everything we do under the protection of his Lordship and guidance.

Ask yourself in questionable situations, "Would Jesus do this with me?" We need to treat all choices as either right of wrong. They're either faithful steps of obedience to God or they're sin.

Stop Three

Can I break the speed limit without conviction or jaywalk on city streets without respect for the laws of the land?

Get ready to toss your Fuzzbuster.

Here's a practical area of morality that relates to the laws of the land. Sadly, many of us are not setting a very good example for others to follow.

Traffic laws, and any other laws in society that do not contradict God's Word, should be carefully obeyed. After all, Christians believe in objective truth, law and order in society, and right and wrong behavior.

This is true of all traffic laws. These may seem like points too minute to worry about, but speed limits are posted for our good. Jaywalking ordinances are to protect pedestrians. Yet, how many of us have dulled our conscience in these areas where we should be examples?

Imagine Joe Christian sailing down the freeway at seventy miles per hour in a fifty-five mile per hour zone because he's late for Sunday morning worship. Disobeying his conscience, he presses his foot to the metal and breaks the law of the land. He also forgets that Christian bumper sticker on the back of his car. His speeding now broadcasts to the world that Christians are lawbreakers.

Suddenly, he sees a state patrol car approaching in his rear view mirror. Uh-oh. Immediately his conscience becomes awake, and the car nose dives back to fifty-five miles per hour. His conscience wasn't dead; it just needed the motivation of a big fat traffic ticket.

The irony is that before the policeman arrived, Joe should have realized that he was doing wrong in God's sight. That should have been a much greater incentive to right behavior than any law on America's books. Jesus said, "Don't be afraid of those who kill the body but cannot kill the soul. Instead, fear the one who can destroy both body and soul in hell" (Matthew 10:28).

Yet many of us speed regularly without a thought of God or a sense of right and wrong. That reveals a tremendous numbness of conscience.

God taught me this lesson years ago when I jaywalked on a city street late one night. Seeing few cars, I rationalized that the light flashing "Don't Walk" didn't really apply to me. As I carelessly sauntered across the road, the door of an unmarked police car opened. The officer said, "You just broke the law. Jaywalking is illegal, and it's for your protection. I'll just give you a warning ticket, but don't do it again."

With an awakened conscience, and my tail between my legs, I continued down the street relieved, rebuked, and pondering my disobedience.

Now, I don't jaywalk anymore. Instead, I stand on my side of the street looking at pedestrians on the other side who are tempted to cross on a red light. As I gaze at them and stand my ground, usually their conscience will kick into gear. If it doesn't and they walk across the street while I'm still rocking on my heels waiting for the light to change, they never look me in the eye.

You see, we know a lot more about right and wrong than we let on. We just want to disobey much of the time. When we do, we can't look others in the eye with a clear conscience.

We especially can't look God in the eye.

Have you let the world draw you into disobeying the laws of the land? Do you rationalize speeding, jaywalking, littering, not wearing your seatbelt, or other common laws?

If so, then your conscience is asleep in this area of right and wrong. If you're unwilling to change, please take the Christian bumper sticker off your car. At least you won't drag God's name through the mud in the eyes of the world.

Better yet, experience the freedom of changing your heart and life in this area. God wants you to be an example of a person under authority, who believes in good laws, and who cares about right and wrong.

Stop Four

Do I fail to lovingly correct others when they don't do what is right?

All of us have a responsibility to those around us. We can either help them to understand and do right, or we can ignore them and let them do wrong. If we let them sin, we are allowing them to hurt themselves and sometimes others as well. The most loving thing we can do for another person is to help rescue them from their destructive choices. We need to be willing to correct them in love.

Jesus said in Luke 17:3:

> "So watch yourselves! If a believer sins, correct him. If he changes the way he thinks and acts, forgive him."

Today, we're better at forgiving than rebuking. We don't even like the word rebuke. It sounds so negative and harsh.

Yet true correction is not negative at all. If we're wise, we'll both do it and receive it. The Bible says:

> Do not warn a mocker, or he will hate you. Warn a wise person, and he will love you. Give advice to a wise person, and he will become even wiser. Teach a righteous person, and he will learn more. (Proverbs 9:8–9)

Loving reproof is too often missing in the Church today probably for three reasons. First, we've lost sight of what's right and wrong in many categories. We don't know what to reprove or exhort anymore.

Second, many of us have dull minds in the same areas as our friends. When we see them speeding, jaywalking, or anything else, we lack any moral authority to help because we do the same thing. We're guilty too, so we say nothing.

Third, we've confused loving rebuke with judging others. We're commanded in Scripture to "stop judging so that you will not be judged" (Matthew 7:1). That means we should never condescendingly or uncaringly pass sentence on another person. That type of judging is evil.

Recently I scolded my son Nathan about a trip he'd taken to California. I thought his reasons for visiting a friend in Malibu were frivolous—going to the beach, enjoying a few theme parks, kicking back and resting. Nothing bad in itself, but certainly not worth lost school time and large expense. Upon his return, I learned he and his friend had given testimonies on a Christian talk show, written a number of gospel songs, ministered at a Korean Church, and done street evangelism with a youth group. It was a fruitful trip I'd wrongly prejudged.

On the other hand, Jesus also said, "Judge with righteous judgment" (John 7:24 NASB). He commands us to make proper judgments of people and actions. This is the aspect of loving correction we all need in our lives. When we're wrong, we need rebuke and help to stop our offensive behavior.

Years ago a leader in my life lovingly rebuked me for a lack of faith and a sniveling attitude. I'd become quite judgmental toward a group of people I was working with. My bad attitude showed itself in cutting remarks and very little patience with them. His words of correction stung me at the time, but the rebuke brought great instruction and encouragement. I never forgot the lesson and gained an area of conscious obedience that I didn't possess before.

That's the power of loving correction. Often people don't even realize they have a problem. Being corrected helps them learn righteousness and lets them know that someone cares. It's an evidence of an awakened conscience in your relationships.

Stop Five

Do I regularly disobey God and no longer feel convicted or sorry about it?

Disobedience to God is a mark of self-will and dullness of conscience. Because right and wrong are so important to God—they're the center around which the moral universe operates—rejecting wrong and choosing right are the essence of our duty as human beings.

We can't live a righteous life without the forgiveness of the cross and the empowering of the Holy Spirit. But with Christ in our life and a conscience that is awakened, we can learn to obey in all areas of concern. This is the life God created us to live.

Some years ago, I had a real battle with controlling my foul mouth. Time after time I knelt by my bed at night asking God's forgiveness and feeling bad about my sin. The next day or the next week, I would fall again, and the scene repeated itself.

One night while I was praying, the Lord seemed to speak this word to me: "You keep asking me to take this sin away from you. If you really don't like it, why don't you just give it up?"

Truth hit me like a hammer in the head. It wasn't the sin I didn't like; it was the guilty conscience afterward that bothered me. Suddenly I realized: I did the sin because I wanted to. I didn't like the consequences, but overall, I liked the sin.

That night I was honest with God. I confessed my disobedience and love of wrong instead of right. That night I got off my knees with a new power inside me. I'd stopped playing games with God.

Does "Consenting Adults" Make It Okay?

Ever since Adam and Eve's time, people have experienced the loneliness and pain of an insensitive conscience. We've come to experience the joy of doing right and the agony of doing wrong.

The world's greatest questions have always been questions of right and wrong. You can't ask "Is this right?" enough as you make a myriad of choices every day of your life.

We live in a world of right and wrong. We are, by nature, moral beings with the staggering ability to choose. Thankfully, through the death and resurrection of Jesus Christ, we can experience the forgiveness of our sins and the renewal of our hearts and minds. Then we'll want to obey and be sensitive to God.

Christians must be sensitive to right and wrong in today's world. One of the callings of the Church is to be the salt and light of human society (Matthew 5:13–16)—in a way, the conscience of a nation. If our own minds are dull to both the things God loves and the things he hates, then we can never be a moral presence for good.

Commit yourself to developing a sensitive conscience toward right and wrong. Meditate on the following Scriptures:

> Blessed are those who hunger and thirst for God's approval. They will be satisfied. (Matthew 5:6)

> Everyone who sins breaks the law; in fact, sin is lawlessness. But you know that he appeared so that he might take away our sins. . . . No one who lives in him keeps on sinning. No one who continues to sin has either seen him or known him. Dear children, do not let anyone lead you astray. He who does what is right is righteous, just as he is righteous. He who does what is sinful is of the devil, because the devil has been sinning from the beginning. The reason the Son of God appeared was to destroy the devil's work. (1 John 3:4–8 NIV)

Are you sensitive to right and wrong in all areas of life? Do you consistently ask yourself, "Is this the right thing to do?"

You will if you have a sensitive conscience that "wants to do right more than anything else" (Matthew 5:6, New Century Version). It's the only way to live.

FOR THOUGHT, DISCUSSION, AND ACTION

1. Why is morality so important to God? How do we know whether something is right or wrong? Discuss.

2. In what areas of your life are you sensitive to right and wrong? In what areas is your conscience dull?

3. Why should Christians be the most law-abiding citizens in a nation? What happens when they don't? Name some areas of disobedience that have tarnished God's name. What should be done about them?

4. Choose one area of right and wrong to change immediately. Pursue right living more than anything else in your life. Consistently ask the question, "Would Jesus do this with me?"

CHAPTER 6

Free to Care About Others

ALL ACTS OF deadened conscience boil down to this: we fail to love God supremely or we fail to love our fellow man equally. Does that sound familiar? It should, because that's always been the standard God's law requires.

God said, "I am the Alpha and Omega," which means he is the beginning and the end. He saw the first wave hit the seashore, and he'll see the last one after we're all gone. That same eternity applies to his laws.

God should be loved and worshipped supremely because of who he is. And because he made us equally in his image, we should love and treat others as equals—all nationalities, all races, all ages, and both sexes.

God's Law for relationships has never changed. However, in terms of his relationship to human beings, he revealed it progressively. In Old Testament times, it took the form of the Ten Commandments as found in Exodus 20 and Deuteronomy 5. The first four emphasize supreme devotion to God:

- Never have any other god
- Never make your own carved idols
- Never use the name of the Lord your God carelessly
- Remember the day of worship.

The last six tell us how to love each other:

- Honor your father and your mother
- Never murder
- Never commit adultery
- Never steal
- Never lie
- Never covet.

Years later, Jesus brought the Ten Commandments down to two commands: " 'Love the Lord your God with all your heart, with all your soul, and with all your mind.' This is the greatest and most important commandment. The second is like it: 'Love your neighbor as you love yourself.' All of Moses' Teachings and the Prophets depend on these two commandments" (Matthew 22:37–40).

In the age of grace, Paul then brought it all down to one word: "Therefore, love fulfills Moses' Teachings" (Romans 13:10). Living a life of love—giving God due respect and devotion and giving our fellow human beings the care and respect they deserve—is the equation for happiness on planet Earth. This is God's behavioral standard, and it should be the basis for all civil laws.

The more a nation follows this principle, the greater the blessing and freedom. The more we fail to live this life of love, the more we suffer in relation to each other.

The previous chapter showed us how our conscience can become seared toward our Maker. On this portion of our whistle stop tour, let's look at where our dull conscience hurts our fellow human beings. God wants us to love people as much as we love ourselves. Only a seared conscience allows us to do differently. Here are some important checkpoints.

Stop One

Do I sin in the way I speak to other people, without later feeling conviction and confessing my sin?

One of our most powerful weapons is our tongue. The Bible says it is "a fire, a world of evil among the parts of the body. It corrupts the whole person, sets the whole course of his life on fire, and is itself set on fire by hell" (James 3:6 NIV). The power of our words is awesome. We bless with them, and we curse; we tear down, and we build up; we inspire, and we destroy.

There are many ways we use our mouths to hurt people. We call these verbal sins by a host of different terms. The Scripture sums it up in the phrase "speak evil of no man" (Titus 3:2 KJV). Evil speech can be:

- cursing and swearing that degrades a person
- gossip and slander that unfairly label a person
- sarcastic humor that hurts a person
- lying words that deceive a person
- flattering words that puff up a person's pride
- poisonous words that put bitterness in a person
- negative words that deflate a person.

Words are one of the quickest and best ways we can love an individual, or the surest and faster route to depress and destroy them. Whenever we hurt others with words, we are breaking the law of love.

Past eras of history showed much greater conscience in the area of speech. Remember the crumbling of the public profanity barrier with *Gone With the Wind* in 1939? That culture was more polite, controlled, and sensitive. Today, America's corporate conscience tolerates almost anything in the area of speech.

Just visit a job site, a junior high or high school, or take in a PG-rated movie. You'll hear enough foul language to gag the mind. As our hearts turned selfish over the past generation, our mouths went into the gutter. People don't care if their language offends others.

I remember taking my wife to see the movie *Top Gun* a few years ago. It had been highly recommended by a close Christian leader and friend. After listening to an hour's worth of constant four letter F-words and S-words, I felt sick to my stomach. We left in disgust.

Unfortunately, the Church also participated in this evil verbal down slide. We may not be as vulgar as the world, but our sarcasm, negativism, gossip, and other sins of speech still hurt other people around us. The sad thing is, we know better.

How tragic it is to hear pastors and other Christian leaders speaking against one another on television or the radio. A fundamentalist minister condemns the local Pentecostal pastor for encouraging speaking in tongues which the fundamentalist believes is "of the devil." The liberal church pastor slams the Christian Coalition leader for speaking against the ordination of practicing homosexuals. The world listens to our bitterness and division and turns away from Jesus.

We need to clean up our loose tongues and practice Colossians 4:6: "Everything you say should be kind and well thought out so that you know how to answer everyone."

Our speech problem deserves serious attention. It was Jesus himself who said:

> "I can guarantee that on judgment day people will
> have to give an account of every careless word they
> say. By your words you will be declared innocent,
> or by your words you will be declared guilty."
> (Matthew 12:36)

One day God will perfectly scrutinize every word we've ever said. That's reason enough to sharpen our conscience and learn to speak only words that give life.

Years ago, God really began a work on my mouth as I meditated on these words of Jesus. First, I did away with swearing and other cutting remarks. Next, I worked on sarcasm and inappropriate humor. Today, I'm concentrating on other aspects of self-controlled speech. I'm still not perfect, but I'm growing more and more to love people with the gift and power of a godly tongue.

Stop Two

Do I feel guilty when arriving late to meetings, appointments, church, etc.?

Being late to an appointment or meeting without a legitimate emergency or some other good excuse, isn't loving your neighbor as yourself. As we pointed out earlier, time is one of our most precious resources. When we waste other people's time by arriving late for dates and functions, we are wasting a possession they'll never get back. Tardiness is really a lack of love and respect for others.

Some nations have a major cultural blind spot in this area of being late. A few years ago I was speaking in South Africa on this subject. When I got to the point regarding being late to meetings, you could almost hear a pin drop in the room! This was so true of the South African people that they even laughed it off as a funny national personality quirk.

Not this night. At the end of the service, many people came forward to confess their lack of love for others in not respecting their time. A few of them showed me printed church bulletins that announced scheduled meetings in the following way:

EVENING WORSHIP SERVICE – 6:45 P.M. for 7:00 P.M.

What this meant in their culture was that people were to plan to be at church at 6:45 P.M., otherwise they'd never make it by seven o'clock! It got them thinking ahead to try to get them there on time. Incredible!

They really needed an awakened conscience that loved others as much as they loved themselves. When you value someone's time as much as your own, then you'll do all in your power to be timely. It's just that simple.

Obviously, there are times when circumstances come up or emergencies take place that cause us to be late. When that happens, all we need to do is explain the circumstances, say we're sorry for making them wait, and carry on. But when we are habitually late to appointments and meetings, it really means we don't care enough about others to arrive on time.

Being early and being late requires the same energy. Actually, I think there's more "stress energy" around late people than early folk. It's all a matter of planning. We either plan to get ready on time because we don't want to hurt others, or we plan to be late because we don't care about others as much as we do about ourselves.

Once I got a traffic ticket for speeding. Why was I going so fast? I was late for a church meeting and thought God didn't mind my breaking the law to make up for my tardiness.

I found both God and the state didn't believe my logic. The state fined me, and God convicted me that two wrongs don't make a right. I learned my lesson and have worked hard since to value other people's time.

Are you perpetually late? Do people have to wait regularly for you? Then—like me—you're a candidate for grace and transformation in the use of your time.

Stop Three

Do my daily habits fail to set an example for others?

Paul made it clear that believers were living letters ". . . that everyone knows and reads" (2 Corinthians 3:2). People watch everything we do. Either we are leading them closer to God through our example, or we are influencing them to walk a lower road of dull hearts and disobedient wills.

This is especially true of leaders who, by definition, are role models. We protect our followers by the example of our lives. If we are not good role models, all we influence can be led astray.

This is why God judges leaders so severely. They must be examples in every area of their lives. If they're not, their bad habits can be picked up and multiplied by hundreds, thousands, and even millions of people.

During the past fifty years, America has elected a number of presidents who were allegedly immoral men. From Franklin Roosevelt to John Kennedy to Bill Clinton, the accounts of adultery and immoral behavior of these leaders have been reported in the press. The greatest tragedy of these revelations is the negative impact they have on the lives of millions. Instead of young people looking to their presidents for moral and personal leadership, they are left to flounder in a vast moral vacuum. This is the sad reality of leadership today: there are few consistently upright men and women whose daily habits and values are difficult to tarnish.

Ted Jones went to Washington, D.C. a number of years ago to work as a page for the Speaker of the House of Representatives. In the higher echelons of the U.S. government, he thought he would find strong ideals, sound morals, and a disciplined environment among the leaders of our nation. Instead, he discovered open sexual immorality among many congressmen, the widespread use of drugs and alcohol, and blatant deception and bribery. Giving in to the social pressure, he himself became an alcoholic womanizer whose marriage fell apart. He left Washington, D.C. disillusioned and bitter. Only a midlife conversion to Christ rescued his life. Today he trains leaders in personal and financial accountability.

Think about your daily habits. Are they a good example for others to follow? If you were a leader of millions of people, would it be a blessing to others to live their lives the way you do?

You are God's representative—a living letter. Are you a good one with a conscience that cares about your example to others? Or are you a bad one, whose habits will fail to light the path for those who come behind you?

Stop Four

Am I prompt and conscientious in my communication with others?

How's this for a practical one? How easy it is to hurt another person by not loving them enough to return a letter, a phone call, or an E-mail message. This is an area of conscience that I learned the hard way.

During my high school years, my father was in prison for a crime he didn't commit. Our only means of communication were a bimonthly visit and letters. My father wrote my brother and me each week; sometimes several times. He wanted to be involved in our lives. He wanted to show us he cared.

One summer, I was so involved in sports and youth events that I failed to send him a Father's Day card. He was faithful to communicate with me, but in my youthful selfishness and lack of conscience, I didn't realize how important it was to him that I stay in contact.

When I realized how badly I had hurt him, I asked his forgiveness and promised myself never to do that again. Today, I still keep the complete set of letters he wrote from prison in a special file—a tangible expression of his love. I also want to be faithful to share in letter form with those that I value and love.

When a person writes a letter, they are investing precious time and intimate thoughts in the value of our relationship. To not write back, or to take a long time to correspond, is telling them their love and expression isn't cherished and appreciated. Most of us don't feel this way, but our actions speak louder than words.

I once led a series of renewal meetings in a church in southern Virginia. One of the most moving confessions during that time was by the pastor's wife, standing before the congregation and confessing her sin of not responding to letters. Her conscience deeply convicted her, and she vowed to never do it again.

Though my correspondence load has grown heavier over the years, and my secretary helps me, I've never forgotten the importance of returning letters. Even if the letter is short, it is far better than nothing. Two sentences of appreciation or love are worth a hundred times more than a glaring silence.

When we write a friend or loved one, we like to be answered. If we love others as ourselves, we will do just that. An awakened conscience and ready pen will help us gain the victory.

Stop Five

Do I neglect confession and restitution to others of my past sins?

Sin is a horrible thing. It hurts God, hurts us, and damages relationships with others. It cost God his own Son, who died for our sins. We can't take it lightly. God never does.

When we sin against someone else, the Bible encourages us to confess that sin and make restitution to the offended party (Proverbs 28:13). If we really understand how sin damages people, we will quickly make the situation right.

The key is our understanding of sin. Wrong choices toward others can leave eternal scars. If the offended person doesn't reconcile to God, they will live with the memory of your sin forever.

Confession is a way of lifting that scar from their life. You can't really repair the damage. The situation can't be done over, but the relationship can be restored or even improved through a new memory of humble sorrow over your wrong action. Looking the damaged individual in the eye, asking their forgiveness, and recommitting yourself to love and cherish them, goes a long way toward erasing the former transgression.

One night my wife, Shirley, and I got into a heated argument. Fuming and fretting, I marched upstairs and sullenly went to bed. Shirley simmered downstairs and angrily curled up on the living room couch.

After tossing and turning for a half-hour, I climbed into my old blue bathrobe and tiptoed into the living room. Dropping my pride, I asked her to forgive me. Quietly and tearfully, she asked me to do the same.

As we held each other in the dark and experienced God's grace together, our relationship became supernaturally mended. Without the reconciliation, only game playing and shallowness would have remained where transparent love once stood.

Never rationalize the damage your sin has done to others. If there is any doubt in your mind, grab your awakened conscience and ask for forgiveness. If you've taken anything from them, be willing to do all in your power to give it back.

We can never erase the past. But with an alive and living conscience, we can go a long way in creating new memories, a new future, and hope.

Stop Six

Do I lack appropriate manners toward different groups of people? Do my good manners show that I recognize God-given distinctions and individual uniqueness in people?

Good manners show that we recognize the God-given differences in people and the various stages and spheres of human life (including racial, ethnic, and socioeconomic distinctives).

For instance, there are sensitive manners that we should show toward the opposite sex. Men should open doors for women and women should let men do the more physical tasks. This shows recognition and appreciation for maleness and femaleness, and it brings great encouragement to those who receive it.

Another example is the importance of honoring those in authority such as government leaders, police, and military personnel. They are God's servants to maintain order in a fallen world. Respecting their position and encouraging them in their duties helps them do a better job. Treating them with disgust or lack of respect is unloving and tears them down instead of building them up.

We should also highly esteem the elderly. Their wisdom and life experience are gifts to us. Honoring and caring for them shows our respect for their place in this world.

Good manners are always marks of an awakened heart. They come from eyes that see individual worth in others. God himself is the greatest gentleman. He knows the unique wonder of each of his creations, and treats them with appropriate love and incredible respect. The clearer we understand his unique designs, the greater our loving manners will show.

Three weeks ago my wife attended a birthday luncheon where a close friend was being honored. Festive decorations filled the home, and each guest sat in a special spot complete with a hand-painted mug, delectable treats, and colorful napkins. No one was allowed to serve themselves. The honored birthday guest was showered with affection and care. She and my wife returned from the party nearly bursting with self-worth and encouragement. They'd been treated to an afternoon of loving manners—inspired by God and carried out by a sensitive hostess with a loving conscience.

Are You Free To Love Others?

When our mind becomes darkened by selfishness, we commit multitudes of sins that break the Golden Rule of "Do unto others as you would have them do unto you."

Our world talks a lot about love. Deep down, most of us agree that love is the answer to our relationship problems.

But love is not fuzzy sentiment, lustful interest, or good vibes. It's keeping the commandments of God with an awakened heart and a willing mind. It's treating people as we want them to treat us in speech, conduct, manners, example, forgiveness, confession, thought and action.

Carmen D'Angelo, an Italian businessman, owned a struggling lumber yard outside Rome during World War II.

Late one evening, while working in his second story office, he spotted two men stealing some lumber in the yard below. Quietly walking downstairs and coming upon the thieves, he asked, "Do you fellas need some help?"

Surprised and not understanding who the unexpected intruder might be, one of the robbers blurted, "Sure, buddy. Can you give us a hand with this load?"

"Of course," Carmen replied, and proceeded to help them load the getaway vehicle.

When the heist was completed, the robber turned to the newfound helper and asked, "Now who might you be?"

Carmen replied matter-of-factly, "I'm the owner of this lumberyard that you are stealing from."

Before the quaking thieves could regain their composure, Carmen shared how Jesus had commanded his followers to love their enemies and do good to those who hurt them. "That's why I helped you load my own lumber," he concluded. "I wanted you to understand the unconditional love of God for your souls."

With tears streaming down their cheeks, both would-be thieves knelt on the darkened pavement and yielded their lives to this God of love.

A loving life can only be attempted with a renewed mind and a lot of help from God. Look at these encouragements from the Bible:

> "I'm giving you a new commandment: Love each other in the same way that I have loved you. Everyone will know you are my disciples because of your love for each other." (John 13:34–35)

Love sincerely. Hate evil. Hold on to what is good. Be devoted to each other like a loving family. Excel in showing respect for each other. (Romans 12:9–10)

Dear friends, we must love each other because love comes from God. Everyone who loves has been born from God and knows God. The person that doesn't love doesn't know God because God is love. (1 John 4:7–8)

Commit yourself to love God supremely and your fellow humans equally. The world desperately needs to see loving people with consistency of conscience. You can do it! His commands are not burdensome (1 John 5:3)—they are life-giving to the world.

God designed you to live a life of love. Drawing from his power and sufficiency with a clear and caring conscience, let's walk in the freedom of love.

There is no higher or more fulfilling way. It's the path of God—who is love.

FOR THOUGHT, DISCUSSION, AND ACTION

1. Explain the philosophy behind God's laws of love. Why have they always been true? How did God progressively reveal them in history? Explain.

2. In what areas of speech are you most susceptible to sin? How do these hurt people? What are you going to do about it?

3. What other areas show your lack of love for others? Do you demonstrate good manners? How can you improve?

4. Decide to be a loving person. Meditate on 1 Corinthians 13 and 1 John 4. Join a small group that helps you learn to love others.

CHAPTER 7

Free to Use Money

I SOMETIMES LISTEN to my car radio while traveling. It amazes me how many secular stations march to the beat of the material world.

Every few seconds a commercial screams at you to buy a new product, or the business report tells you how to make more money. You're encouraged to read a certain business-oriented newspaper every morning—a secular "quiet time" for success in today's material jungle.

Especially during the Christmas season everyone shouts, "Buy *buy* BUY!" "Ho-ho-ho and go spend the bucks!" There's little mention of Jesus as the reason for the season— just constant admonition to keep spending, spending, spending to keep the economy rolling. It's as if we live for the economy and need to keep it at the top of our Christmas list.

Then there is the stock report. How are you doing today? Did you make a lot of money or lose your shirt? The beat goes on and on.

Money. Money. Things. Things.

Tony Campolo, a popular speaker and college professor, rightly says that the Western world now lives for getting more and more things that we need less and less of. Our world worships empty materialism. It continues to get worse.

Sadly, this worship of money and things has invaded the Church nearly as deeply as the world. If we are to transform the world with the power of Jesus Christ, we need to dust ourselves off from the idolatry of mammon.

This chapter features some stops that relate to our approach to material things. Are you seduced by the materialistic spirit of the age? Do you look at your checkbook more than your heart? Do you live more for things than for God and his kingdom?

These are crucial questions to ask. God wants to set you free from the worship of things. Let's look at some symptoms of a deadened conscience toward money and materialism.

Stop One

Do I act like a steward with all my possessions?

Stewardship is at the heart of the Christian faith. Everything we have comes from God, even our lives: "Certainly, we live, move, and exist because of him" (Acts 17:28).

All that we are and all that we have comes from God. We are simply stewards who are passing through this world on our way to another destination.

While we live on earth, we need food, clothing, and shelter. Beyond that, our true needs are very small. Yet the enemy has convinced us that living for our own comforts and desires is the sweetest life of all. We've become thoroughly convinced that wealth is the fountain of happiness.

We've also come to believe that the things we possess are really ours. We worked for them. We produced them. They're ours to use any way we like. This is incredible spiritual blindness. Remember, "in him we live and move and have our being" (Acts 17:28 NIV).

Every breath we draw is a gift from God. Every muscle we exert comes from his energy and design. We don't do anything without his aid. Everything we "help" produce in this world is rightly his because he owned it in the first place. By his power alone it is reshaped and created for human good.

A person with a sensitive conscience constantly reminds himself that everything he has is really God's. It's just on loan to him to use for God's purposes. Good stewards will:

- Ask God what job they should take. He's the Boss, and gives out the assignments.

- "Seek first his kingdom and his righteousness . . ." (Matthew 6:33 NIV). Money and material things are a means to an end, not an end in themselves.

- Pray over their checkbooks. Every penny belongs to God, not just ten percent.

- Be content with the basics of life. Their time and efforts must be directed toward advancing the kingdom, not building a material one.

- Have a sense of daily accountability with all their possessions. They will as easily give them away as accumulate them.

- Love to give more than to get. Paul told the Ephesians, "Remember . . . the words the Lord Jesus himself said, 'It is more blessed to give than receive' " (Acts 20:35 NIV).

Daily we need to remind ourselves that we are stewards of the God who owns it all. Is the job I have truly God's choice for me? Am I consciously using my life to seek first his kingdom? Are all my possessions his? Would I give them to others or leave them at his command? Do I give all he asks of me for the advancement of his work on earth?

Jim Eliot gave up a comfortable American life and promising career to share Christ with the savage Auca Indian tribe of Ecuador. With three fearless companions, he landed a small plane on the Auca tribal lands in 1946. After a brief exchange with leaders of the tribe, the suspicious Indians turned suddenly on their brave benefactors and speared them to death. All four were martyred for their faith just yards from the open door of their airplane.

Their tragic death inspired others, including their widows, to continue sharing God's love with the Auca tribe. Years later, the entire tribe was evangelized through the perseverance of these faithful missionaries.

Jim Eliot boldly stated before he died, "He is no fool who gives up what he cannot keep to gain what he cannot lose." He gave up all the world offered to gain the smile of God in eternity. He was no fool—but a conquering hero.

If you don't feel like a steward with all you have, including your very life, today is the day to rearrange your priorities.

Stop Two

Have I been negligent in paying my honest debts?

One of my greatest lessons came out of one of my greatest mistakes.

In 1980, under my leadership, Youth With A Mission purchased a half-million dollar building in the heart of Washington, D.C. It housed a Christian ministry center among government leaders on Capitol Hill.

We bought 133 C Street by going into debt to the hilt. We were undercapitalized, yet we believed we were doing right. Of course God wanted a place of ministry in the heart of the capitol city.

Soon, payment deadlines came due. To our horror, we were unable to meet them. The pattern continued as we failed to fully pay our creditors. Each time this happened, I rationalized that God was testing us. Maybe he was also testing those who held the mortgage notes. We needed to work harder, do more, get out there and make it happen! But the more we tried, the worse the situation got.

We missed payment after payment. The mortgage holder was mad. Our advisors were deeply concerned. We were depressed, embarrassed, and exhausted. Finally, through some godly businessmen, I learned we'd gone about God's work in man's way. We'd taken on a debt that was not God's will.

It took several years to process the lessons, undo the damage and move on. Today, by God's grace alone, 133 C Street is a fruitful Christian ministry house on the U.S. Capitol Grounds.

This experience taught me some painful lessons about debt. First, monetary debt is slavery (Proverbs 22:7). God

On April 29, 1980, the Washington for Jesus Rally drew hundreds of thousands of Christians to our nation's capital to repent and pray. It was the largest gathering of believers at that time in America's history.

Do you know what caught the attention of the secular world regarding the Washington for Jesus Rally? On the evening news they showed shots of the large gathering, then after the event, the Mall's perfect cleanliness after the event. The Christians picked up not only after themselves, but for those who came before them as well. That impressed the reporters. Good stewardship of the national park gave ultimate praise to Jesus.

Now how about you? Do you return things on time? Do you appreciate the privilege of borrowing an item from someone? Do you give it back in better shape than you received it? Are you aware that the world is looking at your stewardship very carefully?

If not, your conscience has become groggy toward other people's things.

Stop Four

Am I sloppy in my business affairs, or do I handle my equipment carelessly?

If so, you're in for some lessons. Poor stewards reap the consequences of their lack of faithfulness.

If you don't take care of equipment, it will break down and die. Soon, you're spending more time fixing things than being productive in your business.

When you're sloppy in your business affairs, you'll tend to lose things, miss deadlines, not file forms when they're due, and generally give yourself unnecessary headaches. You're simply reaping what you've sown—bad stewardship, bad results (Galatians 6:7).

We've learned this lesson of conscience often in Youth With A Mission, especially with vehicles. By not changing oil, spark plugs, and tires regularly, or by trying to keep a junker-past-its-prime in operation, we've spent countless hours on our backs trying to fix broken down vehicles. It's a huge problem to be on an evangelistic outreach and delay scores of people from ministering because you didn't change the oil regularly!

I'm not talking about lack of money for car repairs because you're stretched thin buying groceries and paying the rent. I'm talking about having the resources and neglecting to use them. That's not only unwise, but bad stewardship. God, in his love, will not let us get away with it for long.

Be an example to the world in the way you run your business. Take care of your equipment and it will serve you. God is an orderly and careful steward of his creation. His followers should do the same.

Stop Five

Do I give to God's work to the best of my ability? Do I tithe?

Nowhere does a seared conscience regarding material things show itself more than in our giving. Money is our easiest asset to dispose of. If we give it wholeheartedly and cheerfully to God, it shows the commitment of our heart (Matthew 6:21). If we do not give easily to God's work, our self-centered attitude becomes exposed.

In America today, it's sad that even Christians do not give a tenth to God's work. Statistics show that most believers give only two to five percent of their income to the Church.[1] Of the amount they do give to churches, less than one percent goes to minister to the unreached and neediest peoples of the world.[2]

In America, we not only give little, but the little we give is spent primarily on ourselves. This is tremendous blindness of conscience. If the Church awakened its conscience in this one area alone, then billions of dollars would be released into God's work around the world. Return to obedience in this one aspect of stewardship would have a major effect on world evangelism.

How about you? Do you give to God first? Or do you rationalize taking care of yourself? What about paying off debts? Do you keep your word? In a timely manner?

Are you excited about giving more than a tithe? That is not a limit, it's just an Old Testament minimum. Gilman Hill is a businessman friend who once gave ninety percent of his income to missions. As God blessed his oil business, he passed the profits back to God. Over many years, God blessed his work in Israel and around the world because of his generosity.

Open your heart and learn the joy of being a generous and cheerful giver. Remember, it's not yours anyway. It ultimately reverts to its true owner. Cooperate with him now, and follow the financial advice of John Wesley, the founder of Methodism: "Make all you can. Save all you can. Give all you can."

Do You Look at Your Checkbook More than Your Heart?

God wants us to use the money and resources he gives us to do his will. He entrusted phenomenal wealth to us as a nation. These riches should be spent to advance his kingdom—to evangelize the world, build up his Church, and care for the poor and needy. Instead, we lust for materialism and use money for personal pleasure. This is a subtle form of thievery, not good stewardship.

No wonder economic foundations are crumbling. Now is the moment for believers to rise up in freedom and use their money to glorify God. Here's some encouragement from the Scriptures:

> A good name is more desirable than great wealth. Respect is better than silver or gold. . . . A rich person rules poor people, and a borrower is a slave to the lender. . . . Whoever is generous will be blessed because he has shared his food with the poor. (Proverbs 22:1,7,9)

> People should think of us as servants of Christ and managers who are entrusted with God's mysteries. Managers are required to be trustworthy. It means very little to me that you or any human court should cross-examine me. I have a clear conscience, but that doesn't mean I have God's approval. It is the Lord who cross-examines me. (1 Corinthians 4:1–4)

> " '. . . Good job! You're a good and faithful servant! You proved that you could be trusted with a small

amount. I will put you in charge of a large amount. Come and share your master's happiness.' " (Matthew 25:21)

Those who are stewards now become rulers in the next life. You may not have much, but what you have must be completely his.

Pray about it today. Commit yourself to be his servant and good steward. Let the world chase its materialistic idols, but let us pursue our loving King and his eternal kingdom.

It's the best investment you can make. It's the only one you'll have for eternity.

FOR THOUGHT, DISCUSSION, AND ACTION

1. Why do you think the world is blinded to materialism? How does it show it itself in everyday things? Give examples.

2. Do you find the idea of stewardship a difficult one? How can you remind yourself every day that all you have is really God's? How will this affect your giving, possessions, and priorities?

3. What are your weakest areas of financial stewardship? Which are you strongest? Which weak area do you want to change right away?

4. Learn to trust God with your resources. Don't live by your checkbook. Make all you can. Save all you can. Give all you can.

CHAPTER 8

Free to Change the World

DURING THE MIDDLE of our generation of moral decline, I read a magazine article about Dean Martin. The late actor-singer of "I Left My Heart In San Francisco" fame was divorcing his wife and having an affair with Gail Renshaw, who was reigning as Miss World at the time.

Dean Martin was old enough to be Gail Renshaw's grandfather. Yet Martin gave in to the cravings of lust and conducted a steamy and much publicized Hollywood tryst. (Isn't it amazing how many nice sounding words like "tryst" we've made up to soften the idea of evil?)

Miss Renshaw's moral choices were bad, too. At the end of the article, the journalist recommended that they strip her of the Miss World title because "being Miss World didn't give her the right to become Miss Worldly."

It's the same thing the American nation has done. Once we blessed and led the world with a standard of conduct and leadership that was admirable. Today, America is Miss Worldly—spewing out more evil and moral decay than probably any nation on earth. We, too, have given in to "physical gratification, greed, and extravagant lifestyles" (1 John 2:16).

Most tragic is that Christians let it happen. We didn't just watch as the train barreled down the track. We jumped in one of the cars and went along for the ride.

Some spoke out and tried to stop the steaming locomotive. Jerry Falwell, pastor of Lynchburg Baptist Church and founder of the Moral Majority, was one such hero. While the press villainized him and much of the Church kept him at arm's length, he fearlessly spoke on the need to return to God and his standards of morality. You didn't have to agree with all his positions to admire his courage.

But most of the Church didn't even bother to listen. We exchanged being the light of the world for worldly lusts. As we pointed out in Chapter Two, the affects have nearly destroyed the greatness of a nation.

Christians are called to be the salt and light of human society (Matthew 5:13–16), not cower in its darkness. We have lost cities, towns, states—practically our entire Western civilization—because the Church didn't preserve the culture with godly salt-filled lives.

Let's look for a moment at how we've failed our world in the past forty years. This part of our Freedom Train journey is crucial to our future. Have you been a part of the cultural decay? What are the symptoms of a conscience that's given in to the world? Here are a few stops we need to make.

Stop One

Is entertainment a big part of my life? Do I spend money and time watching television, going to movies, idolizing sports or other pleasures instead of using my time and energies to advance God's kingdom?

It amazes me how blind we are to the god of entertainment in America. It's a multibillion dollar machine that's infected most Americans. I liken Hollywood to the "Image of Gold" in Nebuchadnezzar's Babylon.

Today, very few refuse to bow to entertainment. It's the drug of the age. Many people spend the majority of their waking free time looking for fun through entertainment.

Though there are many areas of entertainment, I call the following the Big Three:

TELEVISION

The average American gives more free time to watching television than anything else. It teaches us to laugh at God and morals, enjoy violence, and live for sexual immorality. It has very few redeeming aspects and sits in the center of our living rooms as the new family shrine in ninety-nine percent of our homes.

MOVIES

Most people see fifteen to twenty movies a year, giving billions of dollars to their makers and movie star icons. Most films shower us with enough profanity, sex, and violence to numb and warp our senses. Tragically, Christians spend as much on movies as unbelievers.

SPORTS

In the past few years sports leaped to the forefront as a the god of choice. Everyone wears their favorite team's hats and sweatshirts. Athletes now make big bucks, and kids try at younger and younger ages to become future millionaires.

Last week, the National Football League signed a five billion dollar TV contract for the next four years. Idolizing sports teams shows how bankrupt the values of the American nation have become.

We need to stop pointing fingers at these big bad problems and look into our own lives. Don't forget, this test is for you and me—Madonna and Michael Jackson will get their own one day.

How much television do you watch? How much time do you waste passively sitting in front of the living room idol? I personally believe that *every minute I spend entertaining myself is a minute not spent serving God and others*. We once were a nation that believed in serving people. Now we serve ourselves, especially through the convenience of mass media.

How much greater blessing would come to our lives if we spent our free time serving? We could mow someone's lawn, help paint a porch, or fetch groceries for the elderly. We could help landscape the church, work with underprivileged kids, clean house for the handicapped. Every moment of giving would build love and lasting friendships.

Think of the days of barn raising. What a great way to get to know neighbors serving alongside them and helping them to realize their dreams. It was time well spent producing something and blessing someone else. It was even a great way to encourage a child's self-esteem.

Do you go regularly to the movies? What kind do you watch and why? Many have said that Christians shouldn't even consider going to an R-rated movie. I have a better guide: *what's not fit for kids isn't fit for adults either*. We're supposed to enter God's kingdom with the eyes and attitude of a child. PG, PG-13, R, X, and the new NC ratings simply state the degree of sin. Why should we watch any?

I have a friend who watched the horror movie *The Birds* thirty years ago. Scary images from that story still flash through her head occasionally. Once these awful images are in your brain, they are forever popping out when you least expect them. Wouldn't it be wiser to not put that stuff in our heads in the first place?

Or what about sports? Some pastors talk about their favorite sports teams with the same love and passion as they do about Jesus. I've also seen men scream and cheer with more enthusiasm than they ever show at church. This reminds me of the terrible time of the Judges:

> The Israelites abandoned the LORD God of their ancestors, . . . They followed the other gods of the people around them. They worshipped these gods. . . ." (Judges 2:12)

Do you wear sweatshirts that uplift the world's gods? Don't you have a true God to advertise? What about the time and money you spend on sports entertainment? Shouldn't you use it for the world's true need, helping people find God?

America's culture won't change until believers stop participating in the idolatry. We must point the nation back to serving God and serving people. That's how our time and money should be spent.

How's your conscience in these areas? Are you a part of the problem, or will you be part of the answer?

Stop Two

Am I a part of the land's sexual defilement through pornography, fornication, perversion, or others forms of sexual sin?

If entertainment is the reigning god of the West, then sexual sin is the required sacrifice. As David Wilkerson foretold many years ago, a literal invasion of unclean spirits swept across America from the 1960s until now.[1] Their evil touches every home, hurting millions of lives. It's probably affected you.

It's hard to comprehend the enormity of America's sexual polluting:

- *Pornography.* It's now in the grocery stores, on cable shows, and on television. It feeds the appetites of lustful neighbors and sexual predators.

- *Fornication.* It's become normal for most teens and couples before age eighteen. Purity became very unfashionable during the decades of decline.

- *Adultery.* Tabloid magazines stare at us in every grocery store, detailing the latest affair of our Hollywood stars. Most people's reaction? "Wow, this sounds juicy! Think I'll pick up a copy."

- *Homosexuality.* Homosexuals now have rights, parades, test tube children, and access to the military. Perverted, unnatural sex is now a civil right, not a moral crime.

- *Rape and Sexual Harassment.* What do we expect from a nation marketing immorality daily?

- *Incest and Pedophilia.* Thousands of children are the greatest victims of sexual abuse. Most is done by family members, especially lustful men.[2]

- *Venereal Disease.* There are many new strains, millions infected, and over one million that will die of AIDS alone.[3] AIDS has become the only politically protected plague in American history.

It's about time someone stood up and spoke the truth: *no man has a right to do wrong.* So-called sexual "rights" have literally killed the American nation. They are wrong. If you and I participated, now is the time to dust off our conscience:

> Stay away from sexual sins. Other sins that people commit don't affect their bodies the same way sexual sins do.... So bring glory to God in the way you use your body. (1 Corinthians 6:18,20)

Even if sexual sin is now only a part of your past, it's imperative that you sensitize your conscience and run from it. Don't buy lustful magazines or allow yourself to look at someone else's. Don't go to movies you wouldn't take Jesus to. Clean up your mind with God's Word. Be committed to the purity and importance of marriage. Pray for the fear of God to come upon our people.

A number of years ago God spoke to a Mississippi Baptist minister named Don Wildmon to take on the problem of pornography. Starting a fledgling new organization called the American Family Association, he printed a monthly newsletter encouraging believers to reject bad movies and TV shows and to boycott companies that advertised on them. His mailing list grew to hundreds of thousands as concerned citizens joined his grassroots army.

During the past ten years, Don has successfully forced some of America's largest corporations to think twice about promoting bad entertainment. Some lost millions of dollars due to product boycotts. The American Family Association today leads the charge against lustful entertainment in the United States because one man cared enough to act.

We all need to join the battle to reclaim America from the filthiness of sexual sin. We have no future without it. With a pure, awakened conscience you can be a part of the cleansing of the land (Leviticus 18).

Stop Three

Do I listen to worldly music without conviction and change?

Musicians lead the moral decay of our culture. Beginning in the fifties and sixties, rock music became the loudest voice in promoting sexual sin. In one generation we digressed from "I Want To Hold Your Hand," by the Beatles, to "Let's Spend the Night Together," by the Rolling Stones, to "I Want to Sex You Up," by Color Me Badd. The more the music played in our minds, the further our morals and inhibitions fell.

I know. That was my generation.

In 1972, I was in New Zealand studying the Bible and leading Christian youth groups. I was a young Christian who listened to much rock music during my teenage years.

One afternoon some kids we were training came to our apartment for a Bible study. My tape recorder was on the fireplace hearth. It happened to be playing one of my favorite rock n' roll songs. At that time I still listened to worldly music. It was a desire I had not yielded to the Lordship of Christ.

When one young boy heard it, he said four words to me that changed my conscience forever: "You listen to *that?*"

His words stung like knives stabbing my heart. I was the leader; he was the student. Yet, his conscience was purer than mine. Rebuked and embarrassed, I quickly turned off the recorder, squarely faced my hypocrisy, and asked his forgiveness.

The tapes went into the garbage the next day. He was right. I had no business listening to that type of music. It didn't glorify God and didn't help me either. Over a number of years it had dulled and numbed my conscience.

I never listened to worldly music again.

My purpose here is not to analyze what makes music good or evil. That's a book in itself. However, I think we can agree there are many musical forms with either lyrics or instrumental aspects that do not lead us to truth or to God. With his Word as your reference point and the Holy Spirit as your guide, pray that God will help you choose carefully.

Our Father wants us to listen to music that pleases him and uplifts our souls. There are many good selections available within that broad framework. God created music. "Complete joy is in your presence. Pleasures are by your side forever" (Psalm 16:11). Cast off dullness of conscience "by reciting psalms, hymns, and spiritual songs for your own good. Sing and make music to the Lord with your hearts" (Ephesians 5:19).

Stop Four

Am I calloused toward the death revolution gripping our nation with daily homicides, 1.5 million abortions annually, and euthanasia on our doorstep?

America is no longer a safe place. For decades, television has numbed our minds with daily murders and regular violence. Video games now teach our children how to kill and fight, not how to love and serve others.

Though Americans are concerned about violence, we fail to see the sweeping revolution of death that has invaded our land. We think we can simply build more prisons or make it harder for criminals to get guns. But how do you lock up 250 million people? *We* are the problem. Our consciences are blind to the revolution of death. Here are the facts:

- *Abortion.* Since 1972, we've murdered over 30 million people—coldly, cruelly, and for profit. If people can kill their babies in the womb, they can rationalize any other form of murder or violence to human beings.

- *Homicides.* They take place daily in our streets, more per capita than any nation on earth—over 60,000 a year. We watch more on television than any other nation—and we live out our fantasies.

- *Infanticide.* It's the logical sequel to abortion. We routinely kill babies that are out of the womb, especially if they're Down's syndrome, handicapped, or in other ways not perfect in our eyes.

- *Euthanasia.* The newest wave of the revolution. Jack "Dr. Death" Kevorkian is viewed by many as a hero instead of an accomplice to murder. Oregon now possesses the nation's first "death with dignity" law. With America graying quickly, this is the next battleground. If we don't stand against assisted suicide and the starvation of critical patients, millions will die unnatural deaths.

Each of us must evaluate our heart and actions. Do you cry for the 4,400 children murdered each day through abortion? Do you care enough to switch off the TV and ban the video violence—at least in your home? Do you speak out against the growing euthanasia movement?

America is committing cultural suicide. We are killing our own people and rationalizing it.

Why does God ultimately judge nations? Read the words of Ezekiel:

> "The wickedness of the nations of Israel and Judah
> is terrible. The land is filled with murder, and the
> city is filled with wrongdoing. They think that the
> LORD has abandoned the land and that he doesn't
> see. But I will not have compassion or feel sorry. I
> will do to them what they have done to others."
> (Ezekiel 9:9–10)

God is judging a dying America. Is your heart awakened enough to join the battle for justice and life?

Stop Five

Am I concerned about, and involved with, the poor and needy of the world?

According to author Floyd McClung, who lived and ministered in Amsterdam's inner city for years, you can't turn five pages in the Bible in any direction without coming across verses that talk about the poor. God cares deeply for the poor and mistreated. It's one of the largest topics of Scripture.

One of my favorite passages is Jeremiah 22:16–17. Writing about the righteous King Josiah, the prophet said:

> "He defended the cause of the poor and needy. Everything went well for him. Isn't that what it means to know me?" asks the LORD. "But your eyes and your mind are set on nothing but dishonest profits. You kill innocent people and violently oppress your people."

God has a special heart for the needy and oppressed. If we are obedient to him, we'll share that heart also.

The Great White Throne Judgment described in Matthew 25 teaches that one of God's measuring sticks for eternal life is living our faith among "the least of these" (Matthew 25:45 NIV). It's clear that those who care for the oppressed and hurting are those who share God's values.

Yet, in modern America the poor population increases almost yearly, and the affluent move to the suburbs. Our lives of convenience often come at the expense of the poor. We've also become more and more callused to human need around us.

Dr. Louis Evans and his wife, Coke, pastored National Presbyterian Church during the 1980s, a time known for the rich getting richer and poor getting poorer. One Saturday morning, some friends invited them to a breakfast for street people in the basement of the Third Street Church of God. The dirty, run-down neighborhood was known for rampant drugs and crime.

Their hearts broke as they sat with the men and heard their life stories: born into welfare families, descended from slaves, victims of abuse and cruelty, and now living on the streets. Many shared their testimonies of how Jesus was changing their lives. After food and fellowship, they all joined a circle and sang together, "Jesus Loves Me This I Know." Tears ran down the Evans' cheeks as they realized how indifferent and set apart they and their affluent church were from the poor and needy in their own city!

They returned to National Presbyterian with a vision for change. Starting an "adopt-a-church" program, they mobilized scores of affluent suburban families to "partner" with inner city families to clean up the neighborhood, teach life skills to young people, and bring encouragement to hundreds. The model became so successful that other churches in the Washington, D.C. area soon began their own "adopt-a-church" program. Their arousal of conscience still bears fruit today.

If your conscience is sensitive, you will care for others less fortunate than yourselves. The poor will always be among us, the Bible says (Matthew 26:11). That means a lifetime of opportunities to serve among those he cares about.

Is Hollywood More Important than Holiness?

The decay of public conscience we've witnessed in the past forty years is breath-taking. A nation once a great blessing to the world has become a worldly curse in many areas.

Our movies multiply lewdness and violence. Our music speaks of anarchy and rebellion. Instead of sexual purity, we've become the world's prostitute. Now we seek death. We so focus on our own problems that we neglect the needs of others.

The bottom line is we've given in to a worldly conscience. Darkness envelops us. The supreme value of sensual pleasure has won the day and scattered its opposition. America is a worldly nation, and without major change, our days are clearly numbered.

God always looks for people who'll resist the tide and stand in the gap for the land. It's not easy to do, but national renewal can't come without it. Now is the time we must take a stand.

Look at the following Bible verses carefully and prayerfully. Then commit yourself to reject any worldliness in your life and shine his light into the darkness.

> Don't love the world and what it offers. Those who love the world don't have the Father's love in them. Not everything that the world offers—physical gratification, greed, and extravagant lifestyles—comes from the Father. It comes from the world, and the world and its evil desires are passing away. But the person who does what God wants lives forever. (1 John 2:15–17)

> Once you lived in the dark, but now the Lord has filled you with light. Live as children who have light. Light produces everything that is good, that has God's approval, and is true. Determine which things please the Lord. Have nothing to do with the worthless works that darkness produces. Instead, expose them for what they are. (Ephesians 5:8–11)

> "You are salt for the earth. But if the salt loses its taste, how will it be made salty again? It is no longer

good for anything except to be thrown out and trampled on by people. You are light for the world. A city cannot be hidden when it is located on a hill. No one lights a lamp and puts it under a basket. Instead, everyone who lights a lamp puts it on a lamp stand. Then its light shines on everyone in the house. In the same way let your light shine in front of people. Then they will see the good that you do and praise your Father in heaven." (Matthew 5:13–16)

FOR THOUGHT, DISCUSSION, AND ACTION

1. How do you think God defines worldliness? What Scriptures can you find to back up your definition?

2. Why is entertainment so popular? Which forms of worldly entertainment tempt you most? Why? What can you do about it?

3. What two areas of seared conscience have most greatly "defiled the land" in our country? (See Leviticus 18 and Ezekiel 9:9.) Have you participated in them? What can you do to bring change to the nation?

4. Make a covenant with God to serve him and people, and not the lust of your eyes. Watch and listen to things that are "right or deserve praise" (Philippians 4:8).

CHAPTER 9

Free to Enjoy Eternity

IT'S FUNNY HOW a little idea can change your life.

A few years ago, I heard a phrase that changed my entire view of things. I now think about that phrase often and even have it mounted on a plaque in our living room. I also keep it prominently displayed in my daily planning notebook.

If I obey this one little truth, I'm sure my life will be well lived.

Want to know what it is? Here goes. I hope it will change your life too.

> *One small life will soon be past.*
> *Only what's done for Christ will last.*

Have you heard it before or really meditated on its meaning? Read it again, slowly.

"One small life will soon be past." In the total scheme of things, our lives are very small and extremely short. The Bible says they're like a breath—here one moment and gone the next.

Take a breath. Inhale. Exhale.

That's it. Your life—from God's perspective—is just like that. It comes. It goes. Compared to eternity, our lifetime is merely a two-second breath.

"Only what's done for Christ will last." Much of what we do during our "two seconds" on earth will have no affect on eternity. Only the things we do for Jesus—praying, praising, serving, evangelizing, loving, caring—will show up in heaven.

Worldliness won't count. Ungodly entertainment was a waste of time. Sexual sin was only fleeting pleasure.. All other worldly activities did nothing to bring blessing into eternity.

This little phrase makes you focus on eternity.

Eternity. We don't think about it enough. All of us will live for eternity. Some, because of their faith in Jesus, will live in heaven. Others, because of their unbelief, will inhabit a place called hell.

We'll live forever. Eternity is as real as the words you're reading. Yet, how little we concentrate on it. If we thought about it more, I'm sure we'd handle our lives differently and cherish our God-given conscience.

This chapter contains the final stop on our Freedom Train journey focusing on the reality of eternity. Are you ready to meet God? Are you prepared to give an accounting of your life to him that is far more important than any IRS audit you're endured?

If we allow our conscience to be sluggish, it will block our eternal view. Satan's goal is to blind us to these eternal realities. Do you live your life with eternity in mind? What are the symptoms of a darkened conscience toward eternal things?

Here are some questions to consider.

Stop One

*Do I ever sin in my thought life without grief or concern?
Is my mind deadened to how horrible sin is?*

Sin is the most destructive force in the universe. It broke
God's heart, destroyed the heavenly realm, and cursed an
entire planet. Its reality forced the creation of a permanent
prison called hell. There, the devil and his angels and millions
of human beings will spend their eternity (Matthew 25:41).

Hell is necessary because of sin. It is the final destination
of those who never turn from their sins.

Sin is a wretchedly evil act that can take a person into an
eternity of misery and torment. In heaven, even the thought
of sin is repulsive and hated. Sin destroyed the peace of the
heavenly realm when Lucifer rebelled. Sin ruined the beauty
of planet earth when Adam and Eve joined the devil's rebellion. Our sin took the son of God to the Cross.

Certainly just the thought of what sin has done to the
universe makes the heavenly angels boiling mad! Sin caused
all this trouble and darkness. What a terrible thing it is! Those
who serve in God's presence and fear him must hate evil with
the deepest of righteous indignation (Proverbs 8:13).

In hell, consciences are not dull toward sin either. There,
in the chains of eternal darkness, the people's memory of their
sin and rebellion against God is with them forever. They
think. They cry. They gnash their teeth in hatred and self-pity.
They are in agony because of sin! There is no virtue and
repentance there. Still, their conscience will prick them night
and day to remind them what sin has done.

Earth is the only place—that gray in-between—where
consciences are dull to sin. Our planet is the arena where we

fight for the hearts and minds of people. The devil seeks to blind and numb the hearts and minds of unbelievers (2 Corinthians 4:4). God seeks to save the lost by awakening their hearts through the death and resurrection of Jesus and the work of the Holy Spirit (Titus 3:3–7).

If you are to live in reality in this in-between world, you must awaken your conscience and learn to hate sin the way God and the holy angels do. Even thinking about sin should disgust you. To not think and feel this way is to live in fantasy— like thinking that Disneyland is the real world. It's not. We can't take sin lightly. It destroyed God's wonderful plan. Its penalty is the just sentence of eternal damnation away from God's presence.

Do you find it easy to think about sin? Does your mind dwell on sexual escapades with magazine models and not feel convicted about it? Are you bitter toward some person and secretly enjoy dwelling on their faults? Can you think about violence and injustice and not feel disgust and hatred toward it?

If so, you—like the rest of us here on earth—need to see sin as God and the angels do. Imagine how well hell's occupants understand it. If only they'd been willing to forsake it on earth.

Ted Bundy, the famous serial murderer, began his life of evil by reading dozens of pornographic magazines. Soon his mind became tantalized and hardened by lustful thoughts, and he sought out female victims to live out his imaginations. Scores of young women were brutally killed over a decade because of his blinded conscience that refused to see the ugliness of sin. Shortly before he was executed, he confessed his crimes to Dr. James Dobson of *Focus on the Family* and traced their origin to those early days of pornographic stimulation. He'd killed his mind. Murdering innocent people was the tragic consequence.

Seeing eternal things correctly is extremely important. You can't pursue truth and a clear conscience enough. Your life soon vanishes and the next world is forever. Largely, your viewpoint on sin, and your willingness to be freed from it through faith in Christ, determines where you spend eternity.

Stop Two

Can I walk down the streets of my hometown and not care about the sin surrounding me?

How easy it is to be blinded to reality and numb to sin! Have you ever done the following?

You go out to do some shopping. You pass through an inner city ghetto on the way, hardly pondering the moral and economic decay surrounding you. You think you're powerless to change it anyway.

You arrive at the mall and are tantalized with all the stuff. You see hundreds of people. Yet, when you look into their faces, you don't think of them as eternal beings that either go to heaven or hell. No, they're just shoppers.

You stand in the checkout line and don't think much about the pornography leering seductively from the magazine rack. Nearby a man curses. Behind you, a woman shouts at her crying child. Outside the store, an ambulance screams by carrying a dying individual who's about to enter the next life.

The regularity of these images numbs you and you learn to live at a very shallow level. The repetition of horrifying events and images dulls your mind. You deliberately push the sin and seriousness of life to the back of your conscious mind because you don't even want to think about reality.

All you want to do is buy your items, forget the pain around you, and get back to your comfortable home. There, an evening television program can help you perpetuate a life of illusory fantasies.

Sound familiar? We face it every day in the battle for the hearts and minds of people. If we allow ourselves to ignore the reality of sin around us, the devil wins and we do nothing about it. But if we allow God to wake up our hearts and minds, he can use us to dispel darkness in every situation we enter.

My wife, Shirley, clearly remembers a day of her awakening of conscience. She was walking across the campus of a western university. As a college student, she was away from God living in various forms of sin and rebellion. As she walked, her mind was numb to the reality of sin in her own life and around her.

Suddenly she saw a young man preaching who stopped and looked right at her. With great seriousness on his face, he called out, "Repent your sins. Repent your sins."

At first, his words and demeanor stung her. Did he know her? Did he know the things she was doing? What was he doing here preaching in the middle of a peaceful college campus?

As she turned to go to her dorm, his words began to pierce her heart and bring conviction. Yes, she needed to repent of her sins. Soon she returned to church and to reading the Bible. Not long after, she recommitted her life to Christ.

Shirley is a Christian today because of one individual who saw the sin around him and was willing to do something about it. He wasn't numb to the lost status quo. In his own way, and in obedience to God, he brought light into the darkness most couldn't see.

Now, I don't want to scare you here. We all don't have to stand on a street corner and tell people to repent, although maybe it's not such a bad idea. However, we need to walk through our world with an eye on eternity, and a willingness to be God's vessel to bring needy people to himself.

Is your conscience sensitive to the sin around you? Are you asking God to use you in the lives of others you meet? This was the way the Lord Jesus lived his life on earth. No wonder he did so many fantastic things for people.

You and I can do them too if we live with eternity in mind.

Stop Three

Do I have a burden for the lost? Do I attempt to be a daily witness for Christ?

Most of us hesitate to evangelize when we don't clearly grasp the reality of heaven and hell. If we truly understood that every person we meet is either on the way to heavenly bliss or a Christless eternity, surely it would affect our willingness to share the good news with them.

There is no more important work than sharing our faith with others. If people believe in Jesus, they have everything that's ultimately important. When they don't, they have nothing but the prospects of weeping and gnashing of teeth.

No wonder the gospel's mandate says, "So wherever you go in the world, tell everyone the Good News" (Mark 16:15). In light of eternity, nothing's more important. This is one reason I joined Youth With A Mission twenty years ago.

It is an organization committed to telling the world about the God who loves them.

But you don't need to join an evangelistic organization to have an awakened conscience in evangelism. If you get to know God and spend time in his Word, your mind will awaken to the privilege of sharing his message, at all times and in all places.

The wonder of it never ceases to amaze me. A few years ago I took a group of kids to Albania to share our faith and help rebuild a nation destroyed by atheism. In a village called Baldreni, we experienced a mini-riot when our sound system failed and the people began to mob us. A few were drunk, and some fist fights broke out. Some of our kids started crying and crowded onto a waiting bus. Although we were never in serious danger, fear gripped many hearts.

The next morning there was apprehension about going out again. After talking about it and asking God for help, we continued to share our faith in the villages. It wasn't so important what we would encounter. We were confident our God would protect us. What mattered was rescuing people from death and transferring them from the kingdom of darkness into the kingdom of God's own Son (Colossians 1:13).

In village after village, many people came to the Lord. Some had never even heard of him. As we preached in these small farming communities, the importance of evangelism again cascaded through my mind. There was nothing more important to do. What a privilege it was to bring precious people into everlasting life with the Savior.

One eleven-year-old put it this way: "We almost missed God by being afraid. When we got back our courage, everywhere we went was awesome!"

Is your heart concerned for the lost? Are you a daily witness for Christ? Have you given up sharing Jesus with your crotchety old grandparents or cynical family members?

Don't give up. God wants to keep your eyes open to eternity. The more you see it—and what he's done for you—the more you will want to pass it on to others.

Stop Four

Am I ready to stand before God on Judgment Day and give an account for my life?

God will judge all people one day—Christians and non-Christians. Speaking to the church in Rome, Paul said:

> . . . Everyone will stand in front of God to be judged. Scripture says, "As certainly as I live, says the Lord, everyone will worship me, and everyone will praise God." All of us will have to give an account of ourselves to God. (Romans 14:10b–12)

As you can imagine, this will be an absolutely awesome experience. For some it will be gut wrenching, embarrassing and indescribably horrifying. For others it will be tearful and sobering, but the covering of grace and forgiveness will sustain them. For some it will be the devastating realization that they should have listened to their Christian friends.

The reality of a final, all-encompassing judgment of our lives is found in many places throughout the Bible. Here's one more glimpse from the book of Revelation:

> I saw a large, white throne and the one who was sitting on it. The earth and the sky fled from his

> presence, but no place was found for them. I saw
> the dead, both important and unimportant people,
> standing in front of the throne. Books were
> opened, including the Book of Life. The dead were
> judged on the basis of what they had done, as
> recorded in the books.... Those whose names were
> not found in the Book of Life were thrown into the
> fiery lake. (Revelation 20:11–13,15)

Christian leaders teach many different ideas about judgment day. Some imply that believers aren't judged at all. Others say we'll only be judged on our faith or lack of faith in Jesus. But the Bible is clear on this point: we will *all* be judged, and the judgment will include a complete look at our life on earth.

Our actions will be examined (John 5:28–29; 2 Corinthians 5:10; Revelation 20:13).

Our motives and thoughts will be looked at (1 Corinthians 4:5; Hebrews 4:12–13).

Our words will be scrutinized (Matthew. 12:36–37).

Our faith will be examined (John 3:22–27; 6:40).

Everybody will be analyzed and examined in total detail. Nothing will be left morally gray. All right will be acknowledged, and all wrong will be exposed. No secrets will remain hidden, and no cover-ups will succeed. None of us will have an attorney present to defend us.

One purpose of this book is to ready you for that day. By taking this little Freedom Train ride, and being honest with your conscience now, you have time to change anything in your life you're not satisfied with. The reality of the eternity can also be prepared for.

If you judge yourself and make appropriate changes, it won't be so difficult then. You'll already be aware of the gravity of your past sin. Your renewed heart will have produced a new record of faith-filled goodness. Then when you stand before God one day, you will be praised in his presence. Your awakened conscience will not only bring freedom and blessing to your life on earth, but propel you confidently toward your ultimate date with God.

These few final questions will also help you grow.

Stop Five

Will I faithfully go over the points raised in the past few chapters and make necessary changes in my life?

I've shared these symptoms of a dull conscience with you to help you change your life. Don't think they're not important or fail to pray about them. Nothing is more important than the state of your heart before God.

Use the whistle stops we've mentioned to do a thorough examination of your life. Look at your relationship to God, self, morality, people, money, culture, and eternity. Where is your conscience pricking you? Where do you start? How does God want you to live?

Stop Six

Will I add to these "conscience stops" week by week, month by month, year by year, as I seek to please and imitate the Lord Jesus in all I do?

God wants you to grow. Each day he wants to show you more about himself, his world, what's important to him, and how you can be like him. Every day can be filled with change and discovery. As the old tune "From Glory to Glory He's Changing Me" states:

> *From glory to glory he's changing me,*
> *changing me, changing me.*
> *His likeness and image to perfect in me,*
> *the love of God shown to the world.*

You were saved for transformation into the image of Jesus Christ. Today you can do better. Tomorrow, more changes can come. Your throttle for growth is your God-given conscience.

Cherish it. Feed it. Obey it every hour and every day.

> Once you lived in the dark, but now the Lord has filled you with light. Live as children who have light. Light produces everything that is good, that has God's approval, and that is true. Determine which things please the Lord. (Ephesians 5:8–10)

Are You Ready To Meet God?

When Jesus spoke of his second coming and the end of the present world, the emphasis was always "be prepared."

In the parable of the ten virgins (Matthew 25:1–13), the moral of the story was to "stay awake" and not be caught without oil, unprepared. In the gospel of Mark, Jesus says:

> "Be careful! Watch! You don't know the exact time. It is like a man that went on a trip. As he left

home, he put his servants in charge. He assigned
work to each one and ordered the guard to be
alert. Therefore, be alert, because you don't know
when the owner of the house will return. It could
be in the evening or at midnight or at dawn or in
the morning. Make sure he doesn't come suddenly and find you asleep. I'm telling everyone what
I'm telling you: 'Be alert!' " (Mark 13:33–37)

In this final destination of the Freedom Train journey,
we pointed out the necessity of living in reality with an eye on
eternal judgment. It's being ready and prepared to meet
God—to be on guard, or on the alert. It's living a life that is
founded in truth and not on illusion or shallow thinking.

All of us will one day give an account of our lives to
God. If we know that now, we can prepare with diligence.

Look over the following truths and determine to let
them change the way you live:

"Make sure that you don't become drunk, hung
over, and worried about life. Then that day could
suddenly catch you by surprise like a trap that
catches a bird. That day will surprise all people
who live on the earth. Be alert at all times. Pray so
that you have the power to escape everything that
is about to happen and to stand in front of the Son
of Man." (Luke 21:34–36)

Whether we live in the body or move out of it, our
goal is to be pleasing to him. All of us must appear
in front of Christ's judgment seat. Then all people
will receive what they deserve for the good or evil

they have done while living in their bodies. (2 Corinthians 5:9–10)

I saw a large, white throne and the one sitting on it. The earth and the sky fled from his presence, but no place was found for them. I saw the dead, both important and unimportant people, standing in front of the throne. Books were opened, including the Book of Life. The dead were judged on the basis of what they had done, as recorded in the books. The sea gave up its dead. Death and hell gave up their dead. People were judged based on what they had done. Death and hell were thrown into the fiery lake. (The fiery lake is the second death.) Those whose names were not found in the Book of Life were thrown into the fiery lake. (Revelation 20:11–15, New Century Version)

Free to Enjoy Eternity

This last set of stops really brings together the others we've looked at. It's like an advance trip to the Great White Throne Judgment at the entrance to eternity. That final destination of all human beings will reveal our stewardship in relation to God, self, morality, people, money, the world, and much more than we've been able to cover. God wants us to live with him forever. He tells us how to prayerfully prepare.

I hope your eyes are now open to the seriousness of a bad conscience—especially in light of eternity.

In the next chapter we'll discover just how our conscience became so dull and the consequences we could face if we don't travel the road to freedom.

For Thought, Discussion, and Action

1. How much do you think about eternity? In what ways do your actions reflect that? In what ways do they not?

2. Why is earth the only place of "grayness" regarding dullness of conscience? How do they view sin in heaven? How do they view it in hell?

3. Why is a lifestyle of evangelism usually a mark of a clear conscience? What does this say about your own life? How can you change?

4. Set your mind on the things above. Spend time with people who have eyes on eternity. Be prepared, as much as you can, to stand before God in eternity.

SECTION THREE

A Renewal of Conscience

"O! had I the ability, and could reach the nation's ear . . . It is not light that is needed, but fire; it is not the gentle shower, but thunder. We need the storm, the whirlwind and the earthquake. The feeling of the nation must be quickened; the conscience of the nation must be aroused; the propriety of the nation must be startled; the hypocrisy of the nation must be exposed; and its crimes against God and man must be proclaimed and denounced."[1]

—*Frederick Douglas*

CHAPTER 10

Sin's Calluses and Consequences

IF YOU'RE A BIT "windblown" after the Freedom Train ride with all those convicting points of conscience, don't give up. We're all in the same boat. That is the reality of being a sinner and in need of God's grace, hope, and empowerment.

What's the main problem? The human conscience gets dull by one primary action: sin. Adam and Eve started us off many years ago, and the whole human family followed suit.

Dead Skin, Dead Heart

Paul graphically describes the hardening process of sin in Ephesians 4:17–19:

> This I say therefore, and affirm together with the Lord, that you walk no longer just as the Gentiles also walk, in the futility of their mind, being darkened in their understanding, . . . and they having become calloused have given themselves over to sensuality, for the practice of every kind of impurity with greediness. (NASB)

Notice that word *calloused*. It usually describes skin, but here it's used to describe hearts.

When I was in high school, every new sports season brought the need to develop a new set of calluses. Basketball was especially torturous on my feet. It took several weeks to blister the skin and let it heal over so eventually dead skin formed where the live skin once was.

The mind and heart can become deadened too, no longer sensitive to truth. When you touch a fleshly callus, there's very little feeling because the layers of skin are dead. We deaden our consciences the same way. It happens like the physical kind, by constant repetition. When you apply continual friction to your flesh, a dead lump of skin builds up. When you constantly disobey your conscience, a callus forms in your heart and mind.

But this hardening takes place in many sophisticated ways. I've committed them all. Probably you have, too. Here are the ways we let sin build calluses on our consciences:

- Resisting truth
- Breaking promises and commitments
- Ignoring right and wrong
- Insincere statements or prayers
- Confessing but not forsaking sin
- Defending yourself
- Comparing yourself with others
- Resenting reproof or correction
- Procrastinating
- Living with doubts.

Let's look at them one by one.

Callus Builder One: Resisting

Whenever my will resists the convictions of my mind.

We need to learn to obey the Holy Spirit speaking to us through our conscience. The more we resist, the harder it becomes to hear.

Acts 7 shows a powerful example. Stephen was preaching his heart out to the Jews. They were coming under deep conviction of sin when he ended his sermon on this soothing note:

> "You stiff-necked people, with uncircumcised hearts and ears! You are just like your fathers: You always resist the Holy Spirit!" (Acts 7:51 NIV)

After that someone played three verses of "Just As I Am," and they all got saved.

No, that's not what happened. Stephen's words were not soothing platitudes. They were daggers of truth shot straight through their consciences. After hearing these words, the mob covered their ears, dragged him out of the city and killed him—just because they didn't like the sermon.

Preachers of truth beware.

But that's always the way it is when we resist the truth. It deadens and hardens our heart and often leads us to do some very evil things.

One time God showed me I'd hurt a friend by being short-tempered. I'd spoken sharply to a co-worker named Mary, and my conscience really bothered me.

Sitting down on a grassy spot in the warm California sun, I argued with God for an hour. Was it really so bad? Did she really catch it? Do I really have to confess to her?

On and on I resisted the voice of conscience.

The more I argued with God, the cloudier I became. Soon, I found myself in absolute confusion. Did I really do wrong? What was this conversation all about anyway?

Finally, it dawned on me I needed to simply confess my sin. I went to Mary and told her I was sorry for my outburst. Warmly smiling, she said she forgave me and reached out with a reassuring hug. Right then, the confusion and guilt left.

Through honesty and confession, I immediately enjoyed the fruits of a clear conscience. I'd learned some good lessons. One: I shouldn't resist the Holy Spirit. Two: when I did, it created confusion. Three: when I stopped, my conscience softened again. And . . . I got my friend back.

I needed to learn not to resist the Spirit's work in my life. He's never wrong and always a gentleman.

Callus Builder Two: Broken Promises

Whenever I break promises or commitments.

Though Solomon struggled with a seared conscience and lusted after many women, he shared some wise words in Ecclesiastes 5:4–5:

> When you make a promise to God, don't be slow to keep it because God doesn't like fools. Keep your promise. It is better not to make a promise than to make one and not keep it.

Anytime you make a promise or commitment—and then break it—it becomes easier to do the next time. As it becomes easier, you break your word repeatedly.

God calls this kind of behavior the actions of a fool. We should be people of our word. When we commit to something, we should do it. If we're not going to do it, we should not make the commitment.

Breaking promises hardens you. You begin to rationalize. You squirm. You console yourself. The path gets more slippery by the moment.

When we failed to make the payments on our 133 C Street property, I watched this hardening take place in my heart. It was easier to miss a payment the next time. There were more excuses and plenty of good reasons for not honoring our commitment. Soon, I was living in a world of rationalizations regarding our debt.

Breaking a promise seared my conscience.

Be very careful when you make promises to God or others. Honor your commitment. If you break your word, confess it quickly to restore your integrity—along with your soft and sensitive conscience.

Callus Builder Three: Switching Off

Taking my attention off the rightness or wrongness of my actions.

Right and wrong are important to God. He is righteous, he loves righteousness in us. One of his greatest concerns is producing righteousness in our self-centered lives.

When God speaks to us about right and wrong, we should stand at attention—as any good private does before his general—and say, "Yes, Sir!" God is not only our Heavenly Father, he is also our King. We should know that his conviction of sin or encouragement in good behavior is exactly what we need. We can trust him completely.

We know from his character that his timing is perfect. If it's best to convict us tomorrow, he'll do so. If he knows we can't handle it for a few months or years, he'll patiently wait until we're ready.

When God speaks to you about sin, don't switch the channel and take your attention off his truth. That's not only unwise, it sears your precious conscience.

Remember Jesus' example. After arousing the curiosity of the woman at the well about living water, he targeted the woman's sin. Upon hearing her admit she had no husband, Jesus used a word of knowledge to awaken her conscience:

> "...You're right when you say that you don't have a husband. You've had five husbands, and the man you have now isn't your husband..." (John 4:17)

The woman should have immediately confessed her immorality. Jesus was exposing the wrongness of her life to bring her to repentance. Instead, with incredible ease, she asked a totally irrelevant question to change the subject:

> The woman said to Jesus, "I see that you're a prophet! Our ancestors worshipped on this mountain. But you Jews say that people must worship in Jerusalem." (John 4:19)

It wasn't even a good comeback. It was a totally ridiculous question about where to worship. Jesus used her response to point her to the truth of his identity. In the end, he openly told her he was the Messiah.

She almost missed her encounter with God. We do the same thing whenever we switch from the conviction channel to some irrelevant subject.

When God speaks to us about right and wrong, we must face it squarely and respond to him. When we take our attention off our actions, our conscience gets calloused.

Callus Builder Four: Insincerity
Whenever I make insincere statements or prayers.

God appreciates prayer, but only when it comes from an honest heart. Remember Jesus' story:

> "Two men went into the temple courtyard to pray. One was a Pharisee, and the other was a tax collector. The Pharisee stood up and prayed, 'God, I thank you that I'm not like other people! I'm not a robber or a dishonest person. I haven't committed adultery. I'm not even like this tax collector. I fast twice a week, and I give you a tenth of my entire income.' But the tax collector was standing at a distance. He wouldn't even look up to heaven. Instead, he became very upset, and he said, 'God, be merciful to me, a sinner!' I can guarantee that this tax collector went home with God's approval, but the Pharisee didn't. Everyone who honors himself will be humbled, but the person who humbles himself will be honored." (Luke 18:10-14)

These men were like night and day. One had an ego as big as a dinosaur. The other was honest, with a broken, humble heart. Jesus condemned the Pharisee's pride and applauded the tax collector's humility. He knew one man's conscience was hard as a rock. The other's was sinful, but soft and pliable.

Do you ever pray to God in dishonesty and hypocrisy? Each time you do, you harden your heart.

Remember my teenage struggle with lustful thoughts? Every night I knelt down by my bed and asked forgiveness for a sin I didn't want to stop. When I was finally honest with God, a new power came into my life. I'd fooled myself for years and deadened my conscience. But I didn't fool God.

Learn to be honest with God and others. Insincerity is deception. It can fool people, but never the Lord. As the light of your conscience gets dimmer and dimmer with every expression of phoniness, the one who gets fooled is you.

Callus Builder Five: Confessing but Not Forsaking Sin
Whenever I confess, but don't give up certain sins.

Every form of conscience-searing suppresses truth. Some forms are more blatant than others; some appear very religious.

Case in point is Callus Builder Five. It's a very religious looking form of disobedience. What makes it so dangerous is that it's half right.

The Bible teaches in many places that we are to confess our sins as in 1 John 1:9. Confession is a mark of a changed life. But true repentance does more than confess. It forsakes the sin that was committed. An excellent definition of true repentance is found in Proverbs 28:13:

> Whoever covers over his sins does not prosper.
> Whoever confesses and abandons them receives compassion.

Notice the two parts of genuine repentance. There is no virtue in confessing a sin you don't intend to give up. That's lying. Really, it's religious hypocrisy. The devil himself might confess his sins—if he could still run around and be a devil.

Confessing but not forsaking your sins is a dangerous way to sear your conscience. In the act of confession you feel so spiritual, but because you're like the hypocritical Pharisee, the confession falls on deaf ears. You don't fool God. You only fool yourself.

When you confess sin to God, make sure it comes with the commitment to forsake it. God's word about sin is always the same: ". . . Go! From now on don't sin" (John 8:11).

Callus Builder Six: Defending Myself
Whenever I make self-justifying excuses or attempt to defend the error of my ways.

Adam and Eve did it first. They didn't know what to do with the uncomfortable new emotions that accompanied their sin. When God came to them following their brazen disobedience, Genesis 3 tells us God asked:

> ". . . Who told you that you were naked? Did you eat fruit from the tree I commanded you not to eat from?" (Genesis 3:11)

This was Adam's chance to be honest and simply confess his sin. Did he do it? No. Instead he replied, "That woman, the one you gave me, gave me some fruit from the tree, and I ate it" (Genesis 3:12).

Notice the emphasis. The woman you gave me. He defended himself and blamed God for giving him his wife. So it was God's fault! He was the one who gave him this female. Talk about rationalizing and making excuses.

It got worse. Then God turned to Eve and said, "What have you done?"

This was her opportunity to be humble and confess her sin. She could have been an example to her husband. Instead, she answered, "The snake deceived me, and I ate" (Genesis 3:13).

She passed the buck too. So it was the snake's fault! At least she didn't blame God for making the snake.

So God finally turns to the snake and curses him, judges Adam and Eve, and the ice of a chilling conscience settles over the human race.

Adam and Eve began it. Disobey and make excuses for it. Rationalize. Defend yourself. Justify your actions.

It continues to the present day. We all do it.

How often have I sinned, and my first response was to justify myself? "Well, it wasn't so bad! You should have seen what he did!" Or, "I really couldn't help it." Or, "Everybody cheats a bit. It's a part of being human."

A few days before graduating from high school, a few buddies and I decided to leave a "remembrance" of our high school years in the school cafeteria. Buying a gallon of green fluorescent paint, we snuck into the lunch room after school and painted a huge "71" on the center of the floor. I didn't do any painting. I just stored the gallon bucket in my locker and then watched as my friends did the dirty work.

The principal wasn't impressed. Calling us into his office, he ranted and raved about defacing public property and setting a bad example for other students. Then he turned to me and said, "You of all people—the valedictorian of your class—should have had the sense not to do this!"

"But I didn't do any painting, Mr. Kingston," I blurted. "I just watched. The other guys made all the mess."

Talk about self-justification. I'd been a bona fide partner to the prank but blamed everybody else.

He didn't let me off the hook. "Ron," he scolded. "I don't care who did the actual painting. You were all a part of it. And if you don't clean it up immediately and completely, you'll not be receiving a diploma next week!"

Conscience finally clicking into gear, I sheepishly headed to the janitor's closet to find some cleaning supplies. The others followed in hot pursuit.

Yes, justifying yourself is a part of being human but not a part to be proud of. Defensiveness is a mark of pride and numbs the conscience. The more we justify, the darker our minds get. The more excuses we use to rationalize our sin, the further away we get from God's forgiveness.

Do you tend to justify your actions and rationalize your sin? Don't blame it on Adam, Eve, the serpent, God, your husband, your wife, your parents, or anyone else.

Go right to the source. It was you. If you don't take responsibility for your sin, excuses and self-justifying ideas will dull and blur your conscience.

Callus Builder Seven: Comparing

If I look at the sins or blind spots of others in an attempt to overlook my own.

We should never compare ourselves to others. Paul warned the Corinthians, who had big conscience problems, about the sin of comparison:

> We wouldn't put ourselves in the same class with or compare ourselves to those who are bold enough to make their own recommendations. Certainly

> when they measure themselves by themselves and
> compare themselves to themselves, they show how
> foolish they are. (2 Corinthians 10:12)

This is one of the biggest sins and deceptions in America today. Polls have consistently shown that over ninety percent of Americans believe in God. Over sixty percent go to church at least several times each year. When asked if they believed they are going to heaven, the number one reason for answering "Yes" is that they think they're not as bad as others. God would let them in.

Most Americans' hope of heaven is based on comparison. They don't kill. They don't steal. They don't act as evil as some people, so on God's grading scale, they think their B, C, or D will qualify them.

The problem is, God doesn't use a grading scale based on works. The only point of comparison he uses is the measuring stick of his Word and Law. Before it, all are guilty and our common grade is F.

Salvation is not based on comparing our deeds with others. Romans 3:21–26 tells us it is only by grace through faith in Jesus Christ that we will be welcomed into heaven.

For most of my childhood I viewed myself as a good person, especially when I compared myself with that kid down the street. When I sinned by losing my temper or cheating on a board game, I quickly overlooked it by focusing on the sins of others. They did it, too. So what's the big deal? I don't blow it as much as they do. So God must be happy with me.

It was a lie, a deception, a sure-fire way to keep scorching my conscience into oblivion.

Callus Builder Eight: Resenting Correction

Whenever I resent or resist correction in my life.

Proverbs 9:8–9 contain some helpful words of wisdom:

> Do not warn a mocker, or he will hate you. Warn
> a wise person, and he will love you. Give advice to
> a wise person and he will become even wiser.
> Teach a righteous person and he will learn more.

Whenever you find yourself resenting or resisting some-one who is correcting you, know in your heart that you are dulling your conscience. You see, the humble man has nothing to hide. He's not trying to cover his tail or excuse his sin. He knows he's a sinner, so when somebody corrects him, he listens. He doesn't ignore the rebuke. If the rebuke is true, he humbly receives it—changing his life and growing in wisdom.

When you humbly receive correction, you have absolutely nothing to lose—except sin and pride you don't need anyway.

I remember once being corrected by an agitated young man. I'd been teaching a class, and he was offended by some of my remarks. After the lecture was over, he approached the podium and rebuked me to my face. His words stung at the time, yet God gave me grace to receive them. I thanked him for caring enough to speak to me and told him I would pray over what he'd shared.

In my prayer time, God showed me that the rebuke wasn't accurate. But the more I prayed, the more God revealed areas of my life that he did want me to change. He used my self-examination to reveal insights about my own insecurities and sinful tendencies. This led to personal spiritual growth.

You can never go wrong by listening to correction. If the rebuke is right, you'll receive it and become wiser. If it's false, you'll still have a good prayer time and receive other insights. Humbly accepting reproof is a win/win situation.

Resenting or resisting reproof is a lose/lose. You miss the opportunity to change, sear your conscience, and perhaps lose a friend in the process.

Callus Builder Nine: Procrastinating
When I don't act immediately on what God has shown me.

Whenever you put off doing something God has shown you to do, it's harder to get back to the conviction you had before. You're becoming hardened. The sensitivity to right and wrong gets less and less reliable.

It's so important to learn instant obedience. Anything less is procrastination. Around our house, we require instant, joyful, total obedience from our family. We don't always do it, but anything less falls short of God's standard.

Instant obedience is crucial. Otherwise, the habit of disobedience reinforces itself, and the signal of conscience gets dimmer and dimmer.

Once I was preaching in a church where two friends were a part of the audience. They were not normal church-goers but came because they lived across the street from the church who'd invited me.

When I gave the invitation, I noticed that they were restless, under conviction, and appeared as if they would come forward. Yet, when the altar call finished they hadn't moved.

After the service ended, we went across the street to eat at their house. They told me over lunch they were deeply stirred in the service to come forward but didn't want to do it in front of all the people. I asked them if they wanted to do it now. They said no, because the same feelings were no longer there. They said they'd do it later. No matter how hard I tried, I couldn't bring them back to conviction.

My friends hardened their hearts by procrastinating. They missed the "day of salvation" (2 Corinthians 6:2). Tragically, they stand outside the kingdom of God today, watching but not hearing the invitation to come in.

Learn to never procrastinate with God. Respond when he speaks. Go when he says go. Then your conscience will stay awake and will not lull your spiritual life into a dangerous stupor.

Callus Builder Ten: Living With Doubts

When I don't want answers for questionable or hazy activities in my life.

God wants us to live without doubts of conscience. Romans 14:23 says, "But if a person has doubts and still eats, he is condemned because he didn't act in faith. Anything that is not done in faith is sin."

Why are doubtful actions sinful? Here's a practical example.

Some years back I was sitting in front of the television set watching a Saturday afternoon ball game. A doubt came into my mind. *You didn't have your quiet time yet. Is this the best use of your time? This game isn't very good anyway.*

I wasn't sure where the thought came from. I continued watching the game. The thought came again. *Is this the best use of your time?* The doubt persisted. *It's a pretty crummy game,* I admitted to myself.

Still doubting, I continued to watch. After a while, I wasn't sure what I should do. I became confused.

I kept sitting, glued to the set, never answering the doubts. When the game ended, I switched off the TV. I didn't realize I'd just sinned against God.

Why? What made my actions sinful and a sure-fire way to dull my conscience? Because I didn't answer the doubts— and doubtful actions are sinful.

Why are doubtful actions sinful? When we don't answer doubts about right and wrong, it means we really don't want to know. That's selfishness, which is sin.

Sin is not simply knowing right from wrong. We sin whenever we do not reach out for knowledge in questionable areas of our lives.

Let's replay the tape. I'm sitting again in front of the TV watching the game. The doubt comes into my mind. *You didn't have your quiet time. Is this the best use of your time?* I consider the question. *Having a good quiet time is better for me.* I decide what's right, click off the remote and head to my room to spend some time with God.

This second scenario has happened a number of times since I've discovered that doubtful actions are sinful. I've learned to live by faith, not selfish feeling. By doing so, I don't sin or harden my delicate conscience.

Some of you may think: "Man, that's a very high standard! Living without doubts? Impossible!"

Yes, it is, without the grace of God and the power of the Holy Spirit. Yet God requires it. He wants us to live a life of faith. Why would we want anything less?

The Consequences of a Dull Conscience

If we develop a dull conscience, we open ourselves up to a host of negative results. All of these consequences of not listening to our conscience are bad—but some are downright scary.

Slow Spiritual Growth

The first result of a bad conscience is slow spiritual growth in the lives of Christians. Your conscience is like the throttle of your spiritual life. If you protect and cherish it, it will open wide, and you'll zoom down the highway. The more open and sensitive your conscience is, the faster you'll grow in your relationship with the Lord.

A few years ago, I really struggled with being a workaholic and meeting the needs of my family. I wasn't giving enough time and attention to my wife and kids, and all of us were suffering as a result. There was anxiety in the home. Tempers flared easily. None of us seemed to be growing in our relationship to the Lord or one another.

Finally, it dawned on me that I was to blame. I'd become hardened to Shirley's needs and oblivious to the cries of my children around me—even with four of them shouting for attention. I asked God's and their forgiveness, put away my briefcase after work, and asked God to help me be a better dad. With awakened consciences, my family and I entered a needed period of growing togetherness and maturing love.

Do you wonder why some people never seem to grow spiritually? Their prayer life today is the same as it was ten years ago. There's no growth in holiness, maybe even occasional backstepping. Instead of becoming more like Christ, they've simply stayed the same. Why?

Their seared conscience doesn't allow God's light to transform them, so they're stuck in slow gear.

The Corinthian believers are an example. Paul called them "worldly—mere infants in Christ" (1 Corinthians 3:1 NIV). He said he gave them milk because although they should be ready for solid food, they were not. Their hearts were dull, so they were not growing.

Do you want to grow spiritually? Do you want to be everything God wants you to be? Then purify your conscience and open wide the throttle to spiritual growth. Your spiritual bones will get strong, and your muscles will become well coordinated.

But only if your heart is sensitive to him.

A False Concept of Character

When your conscience is dull, you think you are better than you are. You believe that your character is okay, especially compared to some friends and relatives. Cultural Christians who vaguely believe in God due to their heritage but aren't personally committed to a Christ-centered life, are an example of this category.

These people know they're not perfect, but think of themselves as good people. In their estimation, they're good enough to make it into heaven.

However, their view of their own character and God's view are two different things. Though most of their lifestyles are fairly moral, God looks on the heart. He sees a pretense of religion with a lot of self-centered motivations.

His view of their character is very black; they need his forgiveness and restoration. These good people don't see that. Their conscience is dull.

Thus they live in an illusion, a dream. The day of judgment will shockingly reveal their true character.

I lived a good portion of my teenage and early adult years in this type of character fog. I was a "pretty good guy" because of my outwardly moral life. I went to church, kept the Ten Commandments, but inwardly had a bad heart. One day God pulled the rug of self-inflation out from under me, and I broke down and cried over my arrogance. The religious mask fell to the ground, and I committed myself to a pure-hearted life. I saw through the fog.

Obviously, it's impossible for us to totally see ourselves as God does. But a clear conscience will bring us as close as possible to seeing our lives in reality. The purer our hearts, the more we'll look at things with the eyes of God. Our view of our own character will line up with God's truthful view.

False Security And Hope

Many religious people, via a darkened conscience, feel that they have nothing to fear of the future. They have some faith in God and know about Jesus. They even go to church regularly or maybe at Christmas and Easter! So they believe they're going to heaven. A rude awakening is coming.

Judgment Day for all of us will be an awesome experience. I believe it will be the worst for religious, unsaved people who've lived most of their lives thinking they were secure. But as they're standing before God, their heart is revealed for what it really is—selfish and uncommitted to God and his grace—and they're standing in shock as he places them with the goats.

Millions cry out, "How can this be? I believe in you, God! I believe in you, Jesus! What are you doing? I belong with the sheep."

God tells us in Matthew 7:23 that he sees it differently. His simple, pathetic words are, "I've never known you. Get away from me, you evil people." Remember—those words were written to religious people who called God "Lord." They preached, cast out demons, and did miracles. Yet their future was a delusion because they never really repented and believed.

What a gut wrenching experience this will be for those of selfish heart and defiled conscience. What's most incredible about it is this: the illusion of security and peace was for a few short years on earth. Real punishment is forever.

Don't allow yourself to be deceived about the future. You have security and hope if you're in right relationship with God. If a hardened heart stands between you and God, all the hoping in the world won't change things.

False Peace

A bad conscience gives you a sense of false peace. This happens when we confuse real peace with its shallow counterfeit. We're talking about the difference between peace of conscience and peace of emotion.

Only one type of peace demonstrates reconciliation with God—the peace of a clear conscience before God and men. It comes when we turn away from sin and trust our lives to the Lord Jesus Christ by repenting from all known sin and giving all to God. Only then will our hearts be at peace with him.

When you truly lay down your guns and join the other side, your spirit witnesses that you are a child of God. A tangible expression of right relationship to your Creator is the peace of conscience you have toward him (Romans 5:1).

But emotions are dictated by the conscious or unconscious states of the mind. Sometimes you feel very close to God. Other times you feel far away. Feeling distant can be an indication of break in relationship because of unrepented sin. But not always. Feelings are very fickle.

You don't need to seek peace of feelings. They don't really matter. Instead, strive for peace of conscience. It's the clearest human barometer of your true state before God.

That's why Paul emphasized it so much. He experienced many topsy-turvy emotions. Yet, he did not equate these rocky moments with his spiritual state. That was left to peace of conscience, as he states in Acts 24:16:

> "With this belief I always do my best to have a
> clear conscience in the sight of God and people."

Understanding the difference between peace of conscience and peace of emotion set me free many years ago. During my early years I rode a roller coaster of up-and-down feelings. When I was up, I felt close to God. When I came down, I thought he'd moved away. Once I realized I had to stop equating my spiritual life with my feelings, it didn't matter if I felt down or was walking the heights of ecstasy. I didn't have to live to keep my emotions up. I just needed to be like Paul—and keep my conscience clear before God.

Many people today have a false sense of peace. It's an emotional peace related mainly to their life being okay. Since they "feel" at peace with themselves, they think this translates into being at peace with God.

It doesn't. The false peace of emotion is an illusion. One day it, too, will bring indescribable grief and shock to those with a darkened conscience.

Being "Given Over By God"

The Bible teaches that a consequence of having a darkened mind toward God is being "given over by God." Romans 1:21–28 describes this awful experience:

> . . . their thinking became futile and their foolish hearts were darkened. . . . Therefore God gave them over in the sinful desires of their hearts to sexual impurity . . . God gave them over to shameful lusts. . . . he gave them over to a depraved mind, to do what ought not be done. (NIV)

What follows this passage is a list of the fruits of being given over. It's not a pretty list. These sinful acts bring shame and destruction because they come from Satan himself.

When you sear your conscience, you invite many forms of evil into your life. If you constantly turn away from God, he finally gives you up to the deceptions of Lucifer. Lu's not a nice person. He lies, he murders, and he's worse than any villain on TV. His purpose is to kill and destroy. He has only one desire for you: that you lose your soul and join him in the lake of fire.

Paul mentions many symptoms of being given over by God. They include idolatry, homosexuality, greed, envy, murder, slander, pride, disobedience, and death—all consequences of a bad conscience.

Broken Down Health

Another consequence of a bad conscience is broken down mental and physical health. If you don't obey your conscience, your body suffers.

Without a clear mind, you'll overeat, undereat, or worse. You'll smoke and kill your lungs. You'll drink and kill your liver. You'll take drugs and kill your mind.

I'm convinced many of today's health problems are due to a crippled conscience. Without clarity of mind and heart, people often don't take care of themselves. The consequence is billions of dollars in unnecessary health care and a wasted quality of life. For some, it even spells premature death.

I suspect many mental health patients are victims of their own conscience. Either by not dealing with their own sins, or in some cases, the sins of others, they sink into depression, illusion, and fantasy.

Perhaps I've lived a sheltered life, but I can honestly say I've never met a person with a clear conscience who has major mental health problems. The two don't go together. A bad conscience and broken down mental health do.

When you don't take care of your conscience, your body suffers. It's the inevitable result of not listening to God and not making your spirit and body a temple of the living God.

A Bad Influence on Your Friends

When you have a bad conscience you mess others up, too. Instead of influencing people to right living through love of God and man, you lead them the other direction. If people don't see light in your life, they will be encouraged in a life of darkness.

Because men are sinful, they don't need much encouragement. That's why your clean conscience is so vitally important. With it, you can draw people out of the clutches of the devil. You can help them escape his traps and live fruitful and productive lives.

One evening our family watched the classic movie *Joan of Arc*. This brave French teenager liberated her nation through the power of a pure life. The entire French army during the early fifteenth century stopped swearing, lusting, and living in fear because of her example. As she walked among the troops, they changed. Her godly conscience elevated them to a moral state that God could bless on the battlefield.

If you have a dull conscience, your good influence will be lost. Instead of blessing people, you'll hurt them.

Your life can either lead others into righteousness or cause them to stumble down a dark and slippery path. The determining factor is your conscience.

Lost Forever in Hell

The Bible teaches that the end result of a life of disobedience is being cast into hell forever. This is a frightening and awesome consequence, but it's the only just penalty for sin.

Jesus spoke more about eternal punishment than anyone in the Bible. Maybe it's because he knew more: he was hell's original Creator. Hell was first designed for the devil and his angels, then opened to rebellious man following the Fall (Matthew 25:41). The Bible says that hell is:

- A place of eternal fire (Matthew 25:41). The idea is of filthiness, constant heat, and destruction.

- Where ". . . worms that eat the body never die, and the fire is never put out" (Mark 9:48). It's permanent misery.

- Away from the Lord's presence, "being destroyed forever" (2 Thessalonians 1:9).

- A place of outer darkness with weeping and gnashing of teeth (Matthew 8:12). It's black and painful.

- A place of black darkness (Jude 13).

From these and other biblical descriptions we conclude: hell is a place, somewhere away from God's presence, pitch black, where suffering and torment are eternal. This either means physical torment or the torment of a conscience that is alone forever.

I believe hell is eternal solitary confinement; the worst thing we can possibly think of. It's the loss of all relationships for eternity.

What takes a person to hell? Disobedience to God and rejection of his Son via a seared, darkened conscience. Eternal judgment is the final consequence of failing to heed God's voice in the inner man. And it lasts forever.

Hope In the Darkness

These are the fruits of a bad conscience. Four of them—slow growth, a false self concept, poor health, and being a bad example to others—are possible for believers to have in their lives. Seven of them—excluding slow spiritual growth—can show up in lives of non-Christians.

Does this list concern or frighten you? In some ways it should. God wants you to understand the perils of disobedience. They don't come from a fictional movie. They are as real as you and me.

At this point, some may be asking: "What a miserable person I am! Who will rescue me? . . ." (Romans 7:24).

The answer is the same as the Scripture: "I thank God that our Lord Jesus Christ rescues me! . . ." (Romans 7:25).

The Bible calls it ". . . work[ing] out your salvation with fear and trembling" (Philippians 2:12). It's the joyful experience of a godly life—being free and clear from the power of sin.

Now that's good news!

FOR DISCUSSION, THOUGHT, AND ACTION

1. What is the primary way the human conscience becomes dull? Why does the Bible describe it as becoming calloused? Explain your thinking.

2. Name the ten ways the conscience is hardened by sin. Which have been major problems in your life?

3. What's a good definition of repentance? Name two ways we dull our conscience in ways that look religious. How does God feel about this?

4. Do you understand that doubtful actions are sinful? Share some examples from your own life. In which questionable activities do you need to obey your conscience?

5. What are the eight consequences of a bad conscience? Which ones have you experienced? Explain.

6. What is your idea of hell? Do you think much about it? Why is eternal punishment just? Explain.

CHAPTER 11

Good News

". . . If you live by what I say, you are truly my disciples. You will know the truth, and the truth will set you free . . .Whoever lives a sinful life is a slave to sin ...So if the Son sets you free, you will be absolutely free." (John 8:31–34, 36)

I'LL NEVER FORGET September 15, 1970. After driving forty minutes to Shelton, Washington, my mom, brother, and I pulled up to the Shelton Correctional Center. My dad was coming home from prison.

It was a beautiful fall morning. The greens and golds of the leaves were brighter. The air was crisp, yet with warmth and vitality.

We walked down the dull gray corridor. Today it didn't seem so suffocating and stale. We'd been here often, but today it all seemed different. Hope and excitement filled the air of this minimum security prison.

Dad met us at the end of the long hall. He was not dressed in the plain old denim outfit all the inmates wore. He wore normal street clothes, and his face sparkled with hope and newness. We hadn't seen him so happy in nearly three years.

We quickly signed the necessary papers, bolted past the maze of barred rooms, and hurried out the front door. Clean air hit us as we skipped down the front steps to freedom.

Suddenly, we were outside. Dad was free! Tears flowed down our cheeks as we experienced the joy of being together again as a family. It had been a long and difficult time apart. Everything had seemed so dark for so long.

Now we were outside and the brilliant sun was heralding a new day, a fresh season in our lives, filled with hope and promise. After three long years behind bars for a crime he didn't do, Dad was free and clear.

"It was like waking up after a nightmare to the warmth of a beautiful new day," he later explained.

It was a wonderful feeling I'll never forget.

The Greatest Freedom of All

As special as that day was, it doesn't compare to the greatest freedom of all—the day that God saves us from the penalty and bondage of sin.

Salvation is the greatest liberation possible. On the day we ask Jesus to forgive our sin and live in our hearts, we are free from the penalty of sin and able to serve our new King with a clear and renewed conscience.

Free from sin and clear to fly! It's the most wonderful experience of all.

Having a clean conscience is at the center of it. Look closely at these words:

Baptism, which is like that water, now saves you.
Baptism doesn't save by removing dirt from the
body. Rather, baptism is a request to God for a
clear conscience. It saves you through Jesus Christ,
who came back from death to life. Christ has gone
to heaven where he has the highest position that
God gives. Angels, rulers, and powers have been
placed under his authority. (1 Peter 3:21-22)

What saves us? Baptism—which symbolizes salvation
through a good conscience toward God.

Three Aspects of Salvation

Years ago I did a comprehensive study on the subject of
salvation. While writing out every verse—from the start of
Matthew to the end of Revelation—I pondered the experience of the world's greatest freedom. Freedom from guilt.
Freedom from sin.

It was Jesus himself who said:

"... If you live by what I say, you are truly my disciples. You will know the truth, and the truth will
set you free." (John 8:31–32)

Many of us were rightly taught that this salvation
includes freedom from three different problems: the *penalty*,
the *power*, and the *presence* of sin.

Jesus took care of the penalty by dying on the cross.
". . . Christ suffered for our sins once. He was an innocent

person, but he suffered for guilty people so that he could bring you to God . . ." (1 Peter 3:18). That's freedom from the penalty of sin.

The Bible also tells us one day he will remove us from sin's *presence*. This morning I read Revelation 22:3–5:

> There will no longer be any curse. The throne of God and the lamb will be in the city. His servants will worship him and see his face. . . . They will rule as kings forever and ever.

What a wonderful day that will be.

However, the daily practical problem we face is the third prong of salvation: deliverance from the *power* of sin in our everyday lives. That's where a free and clear conscience is key.

The Holiness Partnership

My early Christian years were very confusing. Some of my teachers said, "Salvation is of God. It's free. You don't earn it. It's something he does in us." Others told me, "You need to work out your salvation. Be diligent. Be holy."

It sounded right, and I found verses in the Bible to back up all these ideas. Yet, it seemed so contradictory.

As I studied the Scriptures, I concluded that both sides had a part of the truth. God initiates our salvation and paid the penalty for it. He also gives me power to do it.

But he requires my *cooperation*.

It's a partnership. God does his part—which I can't possibly do. I do my part that he won't do. The goal of this cooperative effort is to free me from the power of sin. The Bible calls this holiness or, an even bigger word, sanctification. Paul states this clearly in one little verse:

> . . . from the beginning God chose you to be saved through the sanctifying work of the Spirit and through belief in the truth. (2 Thessalonians 2:13 NIV)

There's the cooperative partnership. Salvation is a joint enterprise. God gives power by his Spirit and we believe and obey. He does his part and we do ours.

For most of us, our part's the problem. We know God's power is available. The problem is breaking free from the power of sin.

What's wrong?

Keeping a clear conscience to break the power of sin. That's the missing element. And on the human side of the equation, freedom from sin involves a lifestyle of repentance and faith.

Repent and Believe

Sadly, many of us entered God's kingdom in piecemeal fashion. Either lacking a clear gospel presentation or responding inadequately ourselves, we didn't fully repent and believe when given the first opportunity. For some of us, it took years to really turn from our sin and crown Jesus Lord of every area of our lives.

Dave grew as a kid in a church where he "gave his life to Jesus" a few times each month at the altar. At age eighteen, he traveled to Europe on a summer missions trip. When he came home, he got married and drifted away from God.

A few years later, he "came back to Christ" and moved in with a group that was later exposed as a cult. His marriage collapsed and so did his latest Christian experience. After he remarried, he fully yielded his life to Christ in repentance and faith. Today, he leads a fruitful youth ministry.

Dave was unclear for many years on repentance and faith. His life was a spiritual roller coaster ride.

Many of us have similar stories. We are not clear on *repentance and faith*.

If we want victory over sin and grace to overcome the darkness in our world, we must cooperate with God, who will give us grace, strength, knowledge, encouragement, and power. Our job is to live a life of repentance and faith which allows us to maintain a pure and cleansed conscience.

In other words, the way we got saved—by repenting and believing—is the same way we stay saved. The Bible calls this "working out your salvation with fear and trembling" (Philippians 2:12).

So what does that mean?

Repentance

It literally means to change your mind—to stop thinking one way and head the other direction. The New Century Version translates the word *repent* as a *changed heart and life*. It involves:

- Grief over sin (2 Corinthians 7:10). A repentant heart is sorry for its wrong choice.

- Confession of your sins to God and others (1 John 1:9, James 5:16). If you sin against God, admit to him. If you sin against others, admit it to them.

- Restitution to God and others (Luke 3:8-14). Restore to God your love and give your life back to him. If you've taken things from others, give them back.

- Resolve to sin no more (John 8:11). Make a willful commitment to not do it again with God's help.

Repentance is the thoughtful action of admitting our error and turning from it. It's often accompanied by much prayer, reflection, and intense self-examination. It's the *negative* part of the equation—turning away from what's wrong.

Faith

Believing is the positive part. It's turning to what's right—to Jesus—in wholehearted trust. True faith also implies several things:

- Willingness to believe that God forgives you (Ephesians 2:4).

- Looking to Jesus, the author and finisher of faith (Hebrews 12:1–2). Faith is keeping your eyes on the One who is holy.

- Accepting his death and resurrection for you (John 3:16, Romans 10:9–10). The penalty is paid. Sin's power vanishes.

Faith, like repentance, is a thoughtful action that's also done with prayer and deep meditation. Faith clothes itself with praise for God's work in your life.

Now It's Your Turn

In the opening chapter, I shared with you about a special conscience cleansing time. I was shut away in the quiet of my grandparents' home to clean up the cobwebs of sin in my life. Over the course of a few hours, I listed my sins on paper, then repented of them one by one.

I did this exercise because my own salvation experience was shallow and incomplete. I hadn't let Jesus be Lord of everything. I'd refused to open all the closets of my life and allowed God to air them out.

That wonderful day, I was working out my salvation through repentance and faith by clearing my conscience of all the remains of sin left undone. After listing them all and asking God if there were more, his still, small voice inside me said, "No, there's nothing more." Instantly, God broke off the chains of a defiled conscience.

I was free! My conscience was clear!

Now, all I needed was to keep my conscience clear by daily repentance and faith. By his grace and through his power, I've done that.

Going over to the fireplace, I tore up the sheet and began to praise the wonderful God who came to set me free. Tears flowed freely and my bass voice boomed as if it were a choir of its own!

I was *free and clear.*

You can be, too.

Get out a piece of paper and sit in your favorite spot to list all the sins you remember committing. It's not important where you sit, just that you spend time alone with God.

If you've never done it before, now is the time to gain power over sin by clearing your conscience. Repentance and faith are your part of the deal. God will do the rest. That's the good news.

We all have busy schedules these days, but it's vital to put other things away and make the time to spend with God. This may be one of the most important days of your life. He wants you free and clear.

If you don't have a fireplace in which to burn up your list, a garbage can or a barbecue will do. Just dump your sins in a place where you'll never pick them up again.

Here are some practical suggestions that may help you with your conscience cleansing time with God:

1. Choose a place where you can be undisturbed for hours. You may have to schedule a time in some secluded location.

2. Use the Ten Commandments in Exodus 20 and Deuteronomy 5 as a guide for categorizing your sins on paper. Under each commandment, list every specific sin you remember committing that relates to that area. For example, list all sexual sins under Commandment Seven, "You shall not commit adultery." Don't worry about overlap.

3. Ask the Holy Spirit to illuminate your mind and jog your memory. You'll be amazed at what he shows you.

4. Keep a separate piece of paper for any follow-up required. For example, if God shows you a person you've been angry with but have never asked their forgiveness, then this paper will note the action item that needs completion. Don't burn this follow-up page.

5. After writing down everything you remember on your main paper, go over the entire list once or twice. Keep listing the sins until your memory is exhausted. As you write down your specific sins against God and others, ask his specific forgiveness.

6. Take at good look at your life sins. Any patterns? Obvious weaknesses? Major things left undone? Confession or restitution to make? Commit yourself to follow through on any insights.

7. Ask God one final time if there's anything more. When he shows you nothing else, put down your pencil and thank him for his grace.

8. Go to your fireplace and begin to sing. Praise him for his love! Thank him for covering all your sins! While you are praying and singing, burn your ledger of wrongs. The power of past sin is being broken.

9. Follow through on all your action items.

10. Daily repent of sin and trust in Jesus. Keep your conscience clear and free for the rest of your life.

Go ahead. Close the book and enjoy a special time with your Maker and Savior. You might want to begin with a prayer such as this:

> "Father, I ask you to meet me in a very special way today. Help me remember what is not cleaned up in my life. Help me see my sin, but even more, your fabulous grace. Help me, Lord, to clear my conscience once and for all. Set me free! Help me freely live each day in repentance from sin and faith in you. Thank you, Lord Jesus, for coming to earth to make me free and clear from the power of sin. I love and praise you. Amen."

Now go to it.

FOR THOUGHT, DISCUSSION, AND ACTION

1. Read 1 Peter 3:15–22. How does the pledge of a good conscience save us? Explain.

2. What are the three P's of deliverance from sin? Why do we struggle so much with one of them? Why is salvation a cooperative effort?

3. Define repentance and faith. Discuss the phrase "the way you got saved is the same way you live out your salvation." What does this mean?

4. Did you make special time to cleanse your conscience? Share your experience. What did you learn? What did God show you.

5. Stand fast in the freedom Christ has given you. Keep your conscience free and clear for the rest of your life.

CHAPTER 12

Holy Living & the Coming Revival

But dedicate your lives to Christ as Lord. Always be ready to defend your confidence in God when anyone asks you to explain it. However, make your defense with gentleness and respect. Keep your conscience clear. Then those who treat the good Christian life you live with contempt will feel ashamed that they have ridiculed you. (1 Peter 3:15–16)

WE WERE STUDYING a very popular book about God's grace. I and a group of high school chums met once a week with John[1], a school teacher and youth leader, who was in charge of our discipleship class. Sitting in John's cozy basement, we were having a lively, almost heated discussion.

"Don't worry, Ron. God doesn't care about sin anymore. When he looks into your life, all he sees is Jesus."

John put down his book and gave me a big smile. He could see I was struggling.

"What do you mean sin's not important?" I blurted out. "Didn't Jesus come to save us from sin?" At sixteen, I was asking many questions. It just didn't seem to make sense.

212 • Restoring America's Conscience

John tried to reassure me. "Yeah, that's right. But the book says here that it's already taken care of. Forget about sin and just enjoy his grace."

"What about repentance?" I asked. "I find so many references in the Bible about the need to repent. Jesus himself said we needed to repent and believe!"

"Yeah, but that was before the cross," John was starting to sound like the teacher again. "After the cross we entered the age of grace. Our sins are forgiven. Don't you understand?"

I did and I didn't. But I had another question.

"John, I also don't get it about holiness and doing good works. All kinds of verses in the Bible not only talk it, they demand it. The guy in this book says that our deeds don't matter, only our faith."

John went to his mental chalkboard again. I could see it coming. "It's all a part of the same lie, Ron. Law, repentance, good works, holiness. That's Old Testament stuff. We now live in the age of grace. Those things don't matter anymore. All that stuff is just legalism."

Several friends nodded in agreement. More questions came, and more answers were given. I wasn't the only one who left confused that day.

Legalism. That was a new word. It sounded pretty bad.

In the years that followed, I remained in confusion comparing John's ideas and many others with what I was reading in the Bible. The more I studied the Bible, the more the truth came clear to me.

A few years later, John committed adultery with a fellow school teacher. Soon after, he divorced his wife. Apparently sin didn't matter. A few years after that, he divorced his second wife and married a third. When I saw him a few years ago, he wasn't walking with Christ any longer.

I tracked down the others in the Bible study to see what they were doing. To my knowledge, not one of them was still a Christian. They'd drifted off into various self-centered, worldly lifestyles. So much for grace. It seemed more like disgrace.

About this time, God answered nearly all my questions about legalism and grace. As a teenager I had been duped— especially on the subject of legalism.

What Is Legalism?

Maybe some of you have never heard the word legalism. So we'd better all get on the same page. If you haven't, you probably will—maybe after sharing this book with a friend.

For others of you, the L-word has already been forming on your lips. You took the Freedom Train journey through many detailed areas of conscience. You read about repentance and faith and decided under your breath:

"This guy's a legalist."

I'm not a legalist. I'm a person who's committed to bib-lical obedience and freedom of conscience.

Legalism is a catchall word you hear today that goes back to biblical times. When a pastor teaches on obedience, somebody usually cries legalism. Whenever a visiting evange-list preaches on repentance or holiness or gives a call to good deeds before God, someone cries legalism.

In fact, when anyone teaches on anything that is strong and requires effort and response, someone will cry legalism.

It's a favorite word to hide behind. Yet, using the concept of legalism to live sinfully is a sure-fire way to sear your conscience.

The word *legalism* is the noun form of *legal*. It refers to law—what's legal and right. Used in a negative way it means believing we're right with God through law or good works. The Pharisees, the legalists of Jesus' day, believed people were justified by good works.

Paul, the best Pharisee of them all, shattered that argument and became the first so-called grace preacher:

> . . . No one will be declared righteous in his sight by observing the law; rather through the law we become conscious of sin. But now a righteousness from God, apart from law, has been made known, to which the Law and the Prophets testify. This righteousness from God comes through faith in Jesus Christ to all who believe . . . (Romans 3:20-22 NIV)

Here, Paul lists a central theme of the Scriptures: that none of us can be right with God based on what we've done. We can only be recipients of grace, the forgiveness of God, through our faith in Jesus.

Galatian believers had a problem with legalism. Paul's stinging words to them were:

> You stupid people of Galatia! Who put you under an evil spell? Wasn't Christ Jesus' crucifixion clearly described to you? I want to learn only one thing from you. Did you receive the Spirit by your own efforts to live according to a set of standards or by believing what you heard? Are you that stupid?

Did you begin in a spiritual way only to end up
doing things in a human way? (Galatians 3:1-3)

Apparently some people were teaching in Galatia that
human effort—the good deeds of the law—was the way to
right standing with God. Paul didn't argue. With righteous
anger, he rebuked them with, "I wish those troublemakers
would castrate themselves" (Galatians 5:12). These legalists
were teaching that you needed to be circumcised to be saved.
Angrily, Paul said he hoped that in circumcising themselves,
the knife would slip! He obviously felt strongly about this.

There was great debate in the Early Church about the law
and being made right with God by grace through faith. Paul
wrote many long letters carefully laying out the truth about
grace, faith, and their relationship to good works. James and
Peter also wrote on the theme.

It was a hot topic in their world. For thousands of years the
Jews had lived by the Law. Now they were asked to live by faith.

The debate continued through the time of the Reforma-
tion greatly confusing Martin Luther. Though a great reformer,
he disliked the book of James, wishing that he could tear it out
of the Bible. He thought the teaching that men could be saved
by works was a wrong doctrine.

The debate continues today.

We're not the only ones confused about legalism, grace
and law, or faith and good works. It's been a hot potato for
centuries. Sadly, not understanding the positive relationship
between faith and works has really hurt God's people.

Faith and Works Go Together

The Bible is clear on the relationship between law and grace, faith and works. We just need to read his Word and not let other books confuse us. The Bible says in simple terms:

- *We are only saved by grace.* All of us have sinned. The only way we are made right with God is for him to forgive us. That's grace. Thus, the ground of salvation is God's mercy.

- *We are saved through faith.* Faith is our trust in Christ's death on the cross and resurrection from the dead. It is the vehicle through which we receive the forgiveness of God.

- *God's law can't save us once we've broken it.* No amount of works or good deeds can make up for the past. If you've broken the law, grace is your only hope.

- *We are commanded to do good deeds or works.* These spring from our faith and trust in God.

- *Through works of faith we will do more than the law requires.* Faith is not a lower standard of morality. It provides the power to live a holier life than the motives of law do.

- *A legalist is a person who does good works to be right with God.* A Christian is a person who pursues holi-

ness and good works out of love and commitment
to God.

That's not too confusing, is it? Grace is the only reason
we can be saved. Faith is the act that brings God's salvation
to us. Repentance, good works, and a holy life are all fruits of
a heart that loves and trusts Jesus.

At the core of this perspective is the difference between
works of law and works of faith. One of them is dead legalism. The other is true Christianity.

Works of law are the works the Bible frowns upon. It's
doing good things to earn brownie points; to work your way
into heaven. It can't be done. With works of law, the heart
doesn't submit to Jesus by faith. The motive is self-advance-
ment. Without a heart of committed faith, good deeds are dead.
In this scenario, even if your good deeds somehow outnumber
your bad deeds, what does God do about your sins? You may
be "good," but he is holy, so you still need forgiveness of every
sin you've done.

Works of faith are what the Bible commands. To the
Galatians, Paul put it this way:

> For in Christ Jesus neither circumcision nor uncir-
> cumcision means anything, but faith working
> through love. (Galatians 5:6 NASB)

I love the phrase "faith working through love." It's the
one that opened the window of understanding for me. A real
faith works! It does good deeds; it strives to be holy; it follows Jesus' commands. Faith hungers and thirsts for right living. It hates sin. It obeys. Faith acts.

This is not mushy faith that turns grace into an excuse to sin. It's a faith that is following hard after God and his commands, not obeying only to get into heaven.

So a legalist does the right things with a wrong heart—without faith. A Christian does the right things with a right heart—through faith.

Exposing this false cry of legalism is essential for the people of God today. If we push away all obedience-oriented training under the false cry of legalism, we will miss the move of God's Spirit that's coming to our world.

The Key to the Coming Revival

We are in a time of great need for revival. The people of God need to awake out of their slumber and decay of conscience to see our nation and world changed for Christ. True repentance and faith with a corresponding *holy lifestyle* will be the engines that propel this coming awakening.

But the revival won't break out among us without clean consciences that produce changed behavior. Inner holiness of heart and mind must produce an outer lifestyle of goodness and righteousness that can transform the society. This type of full-blown revival occurred a number of times in the life of Israel. It's also happened in many other nations, including our own.

I call this return to biblical holiness after a time of decline and dull conscience a cycle of spiritual awakening. Notice the progression in the diagram below. (In the chart, inner holiness refers to purity in people's attitudes and motives. Outer holiness refers to its display in outward behavior.)

CYCLE OF SPIRITUAL AWAKENING

Spiritual State	Holiness	Characteristic
Revival	Inner & Outer	Freedom
Decline	Outer only	Legalism
Rebellion	None	License
Awakening	Inner man	Liberalism
Revival	Inner & Outer	Freedom

Notice that in true revival the Church is righteous in heart and lifestyle. In this spiritual state of *freedom*, the heart is right with God, and the outer conduct matches the inner commitment. This is a full-blown awakening with right attitudes and actions.

As a revival begins to decline, the first thing to go is the purity of heart. Believers leave their first love and faith dies. All that's left of righteousness is the outer behavior learned during the true season of revival. This is the spiritual state of *legalism*.

As hearts get further from God, even the outer standards of righteousness crumble. Casting off the hypocrisy of legalism, the new generation rebels against any form of righteousness. Now we're in rebellion against God in heart *and* lifestyle. This spiritual state becomes nothing but *license* to do anything we choose. We're now at rock bottom.

In desperation, people begin to pray and God begins to awaken his people. As they respond, renewal blossoms in the heart as God restores faith. At the beginning of the awakening, the emphasis on righteousness is clearly that of the heart. If it does not progress further, this spiritual state produces *liberalism*. Hearts come back to God, but outer conduct still contradicts the principles of his Word.

As the awakening comes back to a state of true revival, rekindled hearts begin applying their faith to every aspect of their outer lives. We're now back to a faith that is working by love, a heart purity that shows itself in good works and deeds. We're back to the spiritual state of freedom.

If not maintained, decline sets in, and the cycle begins to repeat itself.

To understand this cycle better, let's look at the historical example we began with in Chapter One.

During the latter years of Charles Finney's life (the late 1850s and 1860s), America experienced the Great Revival. Thousands of people turned their hearts back to God. The nation returned to many outer forms of righteousness in conduct and morals. It was a time of inner and outer righteousness that brought the nation great spiritual freedom. It lasted for many years, even during the trauma of the Civil War.

After the war, the revival ended; people began to stray from their renewed faith. The inner light of many lives began to go out. What was left was the outer righteousness: good conduct, dress, morals, and family life. These things were a restraint on evil in society, but the motive was lost. Over time, the principles simply became a legalistic relic of a former period.

After two world wars helped keep the nation from fast decline, the bottom began to drop out. Up rose a generation of young people who looked at the legalistic morals of their parents and grandparents and decided it wasn't real. They were right. It was hypocrisy.

The 1960s brought a full-blown rebellion against all outer forms of morality. With defiant hearts and immoral lifestyles, the hippie generation wallowed in licentiousness, killing the remaining outer vestiges of goodness.

By the late sixties and early seventies, God began to pour out his Spirit through the Jesus revolution, the charismatic renewal, and worldwide Pentecostal revival. As young people gave their hearts back to Christ, the emphasis was inner purity.

Soon churches saw long-haired, dirty-clothed Jesus-people sitting in their pews. Their hearts were right, but they retained the outer badges of rebellion. This awakening produced youth with a heart love for Jesus, but with a morally liberal lifestyle. Many cried of legalism when anyone talked about outer conduct.

So the awakening didn't grow into a full and true revival. Hearts were touched, but not enough to change a nation. Because of this incomplete cleansing, the nation continued its slide into loose morals and outer unrighteousness via a dull conscience.

The revival was still born.

The Stage Is Set

Our world today desperately needs a full-blown awakening of God's Spirit. Bloodshed and despair reach new record heights. I wonder if the Pre-Flood world could have been any worse. In developing countries, poverty is rampant and billions of people live without Christ. In the Western world, the rapid decay of a once-Christian conscience, has left us spiritually and morally bankrupt and economically poised for judgment. The darkness seems blacker by the day.

Yet, God's light is beginning to shine. In Eastern Europe, the former Soviet states, parts of Africa, Latin America, and the Pacific Rim and Asia, people are awakening to the building crescendo of God's assault on the darkness.

What's going to happen in America? Will the light triumph, or the darkness snuff it out? Only God really knows.

One thing is certain: *there has never been a more critical time for God's people to wake up.* It is high time for believers to arise and shine the light of Jesus Christ into every dark area.

That can only take place through consciences awakened and sensitive to God's heart and mind. To attack the darkness, we must be clear minded and free from sin. We must have renewed hearts and minds guiding us in obedience and sensitivity to his commands.

It's time for another awakening of conscience. It happened before. It can happen again.

America's First Great Awakening

Two hundred fifty years ago, the world was going through a time of great change. The American colonies would soon become a nation. European powers were constantly at war. Public morals were slipping. It was a confusing period with much uncertainty and stress.

Suddenly, a spiritual light began to shine. Starting in New England and radiating across the colonies, it crossed the Atlantic and graced the shores of England with its power.

Ministers began to preach the gospel with power. People began to pray in concert for the darkness to be reversed. God heard their prayers and answered that generation's needs. A widespread cultural revival, known to history as the Great Awakening, dawned upon our shores and in other parts of the world.

It began in December 1734 when Jonathan Edwards, a pastor in Northampton, Massachusetts, began to preach to his community. Joseph Tracy, the first historian of the awakening, described the spiritual climate of the day in these words: "Revivals had become less frequent and powerful . . . The difference between the church and the world was vanishing . . . The growing laxness of morals was invading the church . . . The hold of truth on the consciences of men was sadly diminished."[2]

With an awakened heart to the awfulness of sin, Edwards preached and prayed for his town to come back to Christ. God began to move. By the end of the year, nearly eight hundred out of the town's twelve hundred citizens turned to the Lord. By March of 1735, the revival began to spread.[3]

Serious Christians

In America's first awakening of conscience, the Christians got serious with God. The dirt of sin needed to be cleaned up.

Throughout Massachusetts, God used the labors of Jonathan Edwards, and especially the many visits of British evangelist George Whitefield, to awaken hearts.

In Plymouth, the former home of the Pilgrims, Joseph Tracy gave this incredible account:

> There appeared some serious Christians among us that had the things of God at heart, who great- ly bewailed the growth of impiety, profaneness, Sabbath-breaking, gaming, tavern haunting,

intemperance, and other evils ...We were sensible
of an awful degeneracy and kept days of fasting and
prayer. After this, for some months together, you
should scarcely see anybody at the taverns ... The
children forsook their play in the streets, and per-
sons of all denominations ... gave themselves to
reading the Word of God, and other books of
devotion, to meditation, prayer, conference, and
other religious exercises, and refrained from their
customary vices. And many that lived at a distance
being acquainted with the town in its former state,
coming hither, beheld it now with admiration, saying, "Surely the fear of God is in this place."[4]

What incredible change came to Plymouth as serious
Christians pursued the awakening and moral change of their
community! Wouldn't you like to see the same in your hometown? Does God want you to be one of the serious Christians
who helps make it happen?

In a town called Taunton, Rev. Josiah Crocker proclaimed God's Word. People "were convinced of their sins,
original and actual, having their sins set in order before their
eyes in a clear and convincing light."[5] God was aiming at the
hearts and consciences of the people. How desperately we
need that type of preaching today.

In Gloucester, the revival hit children in force. Tracy
described, "And there was poured down a spirit of prayer upon
young and old, especially the younger sort and children of five,
six, seven years and upward would pray to admiration."[6]

In Boston, the Goliath of New England, crowds up to
thirty thousand came to hear George Whitefield and others

preach. Thousands were converted, and the moral climate changed. People remarked that George Whitefield's voice resonated in the hushed stillness for up to a mile away.[7]

Aiming At Hearts and Consciences

All across the American colonies, the light of God's truth grew in intensity.

In New Jersey, Gilbert Tennent's preaching brought many to the Lord:

> He seemed to have no regard to please the eyes of his hearers . . . nor their ears . . . but to aim directly at the hearts and consciences. The searching nature of his ministry, that was the principal means of their conviction—his laying open their many vain and secret shifts and refuges, counterfeit resemblances of grace, delusive and damning hopes, their utter impotence and impending danger of destruction.[8]

Now this was real preaching, aimed at the conscience. In Connecticut, Christians stopped playing around:

> They turned their meetings for vain mirth into meetings for prayer, conference, and reading books of piety. They not only behaved soberly, but took pains to dissuade others from levity and frothy conversation.[9]

The New Hampshire ministers preached every day on the streets together and fasted monthly. The effects of the awakening rid the town of cursing and swearing, while restoring values such as honoring the Sabbath, restoring family worship, and making restitution for stolen goods.

George Whitefield preached throughout Pennsylvania in many towns and cities. American statesmen such as Benjamin Franklin were deeply affected by the power of the revival.

And in Virginia, God used the Rev. Samuel Davies and others to awaken the Church: "The people of God were refreshed, and sundry careless sinners were awakened. Some who had confided before in their moral conduct and religious duties were convinced of the depravity of their nature, and the necessity of being renewed in the spirit of their mind."[10]

The Lasting Fruit of Revival

The results of America's first spiritual awakening lasted many decades. Not only did it stop an accelerating cultural decline, but it reestablished a foundation of righteousness upon which the new nation would soon be built.

In New England alone, there were up to fifty thousand converts. This represented twenty percent of the entire population. One hundred fifty Congregational churches organized in less than twenty years. Baptist churches increased. The number of Presbyterian ministers doubled. Also, great numbers of church attendees converted. Quoting Joseph Tracy again, "In some cases the revival seems to have been wholly within the church, and to have resulted in the conversion of nearly all the members."[11]

The revival spurred on Christian education, producing schools such as Princeton and Dartmouth. It produced a large increase in the number of ministers and a tremendous interest in missions.

The Great Awakening enhanced the cause of religious liberty begun by the Pilgrims and strengthened the nation toward independence. Without the revival's impact, the birth of the United States of America might have been quite different.

It Can Happen Again

We need another revival today. With the size of our nation and world, and the hopelessness of the landscape we're facing, that awakening needs to be much greater than America's first visitation from God. Christian leaders and the media must lead the way, using their influence to wake up the culture.

We need to learn to listen to our consciences and treat them like the prize possession that they are. We need to awaken and guard them with all diligence.

We need to get rid of our dull conscience:

- In relationship to God, our Lord and King.
- By taking care of ourselves, because we are made in his image.
- Through becoming sensitive to right and wrong.
- By loving people as God does.
- Through being good stewards of the things God has given us, rejecting the lies of materialism and greed.
- By turning away from worldliness and by impacting our culture with those things that are right.
- Through never forgetting that eternity looms.

We must understand the many ways our conscience can become numb and darkened. Each of us needs to cast off these ways, and not resist or quench the work of God's Spirit in our lives.

We must allow God to free and clear our conscience from the stains and guilt of sin. We must pursue a holy life and not cry foul to God's call to obedience and right living.

Time to Arise and Shine

Finally, we need to go on the offensive to expose the darkness around us with the light of a Christ-centered life. We need to pray, march, write, run for office, train our families, serve the needy—do all we can to reform our culture. God wants us to conquer the darkness with a clear and obedient conscience. That's what Jesus died for. If we don't win in our generation, at least we can sow seeds for victory in the next.

Chuck Colson gave the keynote address at the dedication of Focus on the Family's new headquarters in Colorado. The title of his message was "Where Did Our Conscience Go?" Here was his stirring conclusion:

> Some say the culture war is over. We've had our day, and the moral conservatives have lost. Well, we can all see signs of darkness. But I have news for anyone who thinks the culture war is over: Our God reigns! The God of Abraham, Isaac, and Jacob is on the throne, and his purposes cannot be thwarted or frustrated. All he requires of his people is duty and obedience. It may be possible to save this culture yet. But our first task is to be obedient to God's call . . . Let people see the love of God in

your life. And then on that glorious day, the Lord
will say, "Well done, good and faithful servant."[12]

Charles Finney, a hero from the past century, said it with
thundering clarity:

> I pray you let us probe the consciences of our
> hearers; let us thunder forth the law and the
> Gospel of God until our voices reach the capital of
> this nation . . . Away with this milk-and-water
> preaching of a love of Christ that has no holiness
> or moral discrimination in it . . . If immorality pre-
> vails in the land, the fault is ours in a great degree.
> If there is a decay of conscience, the pulpit is
> responsible for it. Let us not ignore this fact my
> dear brethren, but let us lay it to heart and be
> thoroughly awake to our responsibility in respect
> to the morals of this nation.[13]

Another hero, the Apostle Paul, put it this way:

> For you were once darkness, but now you are light
> in the Lord. Live as children of light (for the fruit
> of the light consists in all goodness, righteousness
> and truth) and find out what pleases the Lord.
> Have nothing to do with the fruitless deeds of
> darkness, but rather expose them. For it is shame-
> ful even to mention what the disobedient do in
> secret. But everything exposed by the light be-
> comes visible for it is light that makes everything
> visible. This is why it is said: "Wake up, O sleeper,
> rise from the dead, and Christ will shine on you."
> (Ephesians 5:8-14 NIV)

And the greatest hero of all time, the Lord Jesus Christ, said it the best:

> "You are the light of the world. A city on a hill cannot be hidden. Neither do people light a lamp and put it under a bowl. Instead they put it on its stand, and it gives light to everyone in the house. In the same way, let your light shine before men that they may see your good deeds and praise your Father in heaven." (Matthew 5:14-16 NIV)

It is time to wake up and change our nation. With steel wills, blazing consciences, and passionate emotions we must parachute into our culture as spiritual marines who've come to reclaim the territory. No other force can do it. Only God's people know where the light switch is. We must flip it on in our own lives then turn on the floodlights.

The entrance of Auschwitz, the devilish Nazi concentration camp, displays the words of Adolph Hitler: "I want to raise a generation devoid of conscience." He succeeded for a few years. Then the civilized world awoke and crushed the heavy hand of the Third Reich, ending his reign of darkness.

Today, other forces come against us with the same goal of destroying the conscience of our nation. How will we respond?

I don't know your choice, but I want to help raise up a generation that possesses a good conscience before God.

Now it's your turn.

Restoring America's conscience will require a renewal of clear-conscience Christianity. That means you and me. We don't need the majority of the nation—just a committed minority that can help steer the ship in the right direction.

Without an awakening in the Church, our entire civilization may be doomed to extinction.

Join the host of voices that are calling our nation to repentance. Say to yourself and those you influence what John the Baptist proclaimed to his generation:

> "Do those things that prove that you have turned
> to God and have changed the way you think and
> act." (Luke 3:8)

You can be a part of the John the Baptist generation that prepares the way for the coming King. You can do it if your conscience is clean. Then your good and caring actions will give you a place of leadership in the coming global revival.

Begin in your own heart and life. Be one of God's heroes by overcoming the darkness with a clear and sensitive conscience. As Esther of old, maybe it's true of us:

> "Who knows whether you have come to the king-
> dom for such a time as this?" (Esther 4:14 NKJV)

FOR THOUGHT, DISCUSSION, AND ACTION

1. What is legalism? In what areas of your life do you tend to be legalistic? Do you ever use the excuse of "avoiding legalism" to not live a holy life?

2. What is the biblical relationship between faith and works? Are "faith works" optional in the life of a believer?

3. Give examples of spiritual cycles in the Bible. Discuss their movement from revival, to decline, to rebellion, to awakening, and back to revival. What can we learn from them?

4. What happened during the Great Awakening? What were the keys to success? What were its lasting results?

5. Are you a serious Christian? Why or why not? How can you shine your light more effectively into the culture?

6. Commit to being a part of the awakened conscience generation. Stay clean. Overcome the darkness. Arise and shine!

NOTES

Chapter One
AN AWAKENING OF CONSCIENCE

1. George Washington in *The Book of Virtues* by William J. Bennett (New York: Simon & Schuster, 1993), p. 78.
2. Noah Webster, *Noah Webster's First Edition of an American Dictionary of the English Language* (New York: Foundation For American Christian Education, 1967).
3. Chuck Colson, "Where Did Our Conscience Go?" as reprinted in *Focus on the Family* Magazine (January 1994) pp. 12–13.
4. Verna M. Hall, *The Christian History of the Constitution of the United States of America* (New York: The Foundation for American Education, 1960) p. 51.
5. Samuel Adams, "The Rights of the Colonists," (November 1772). In *The Christian History of the Constitution of the United States of America* (San Francisco: The Foundation for American Christian Education, 1975) p. 365.
6. Ibid., p. 248a.
7. John S. Tompkins, "Our Kindest City," *Reader's Digest* (July 1994) p. 55.
8. Charles Finney, "The Seared Conscience," a sermon published in 1865 by the *Oberlin Evangelist*.
9. Ibid.
10. *America's Great Revivals* (Minneapolis: Dimension Books, 1976) pp. 64–65.

11. Ibid., p. 68

12. Ibid., p. 69

Chapter Two
DECAY OF CONSCIENCE

1. Chuck Colson, "Where Did Our Conscience Go?" as reprinted in *Focus on the Family* Magazine (January 1994).

2. Alexis de Tocqueville in his epic work on the founding of the United States entitled *Democracy in America*.

3. William J. Bennett, *The Index of Leading Cultural Indicators Newsletter*, 1993, p. 13.

4. Real name is withheld. Tom died May 23, 1996 at the age of 39.

5. *Focus on the Family* magazine, "In Defense Of A Little Virginity," reprinted in the *Seattle Post-Intelligencer*, 19 May 1993.

6. Ibid.

7. David Wilkerson, *Set The Trumpet To Thy Mouth* (New York: World Challenge, 1985).

8. William J. Bennett, *The Index of Leading Cultural Indicators*, 1993, p. 19.

9. Ibid.

10. Ibid., p. 17

11. Columbia University study, 1986.

12. Dan Rather, *CBS Evening News*.

13. William J. Bennett, *The Index of Leading Cultural Indicators*, 1993, p. 10.

14. Ibid., p. 11.

15. Ibid., p. 12.

16. *Focus on the Family* magazine, "In Defense Of A Little Virginity," reprinted in the *Seattle Post-Intelligencer*, 19 May 1993.

17. William J. Bennett, *The Index of Leading Cultural Indicators*, 1993, p. 2.
18. *The Christian News Brief* 2.1 (February 1992).
19. Ibid.
20. Charles G. Finney, *Power From On High* (Minneapolis: Bethany Fellowship, 1979), p. 68.
21. Joseph Tracy, *The Great Awakening* (New York: Russell & Russell, first published in 1842), p. 35.
22. James Reichley, *Religion In American Public Life* (Washington, D.C.: The Brookings Institution, 1985).
23. A three-day spiritual awakening weekend sponsored by Youth With A Mission Renewal Ministries. For further information on attending or scheduling a seminar in your area, please turn to page 238.
24. *U.S. News and World Report,* March 1994.
25. Reported in *The Sun* newspaper, Bremerton, WA, 4 June 1996, page A1
26. *Focus on the Family* magazine, "In Defense Of A Little Virginity," reprinted in the *Seattle Post-Intelligencer,* 19 May 1993.
27. William J. Bennett, *The Index of Leading Cultural Indicators,* 1993, p. 13.
28. Columbia University studies, 1989 and 1991.
29. Corrections were acknowledged in November 1992—after the presidential election—in a number of major newspapers including the *Washington Post* and the *New York Times.*
30. William J. Bennett, *The Index of Leading Cultural Indicators,* 1993, p. 20.
31. Ibid., p. 20.
32. Ibid., p. 20.
33. *Bremerton Sun,* 20 May 1996, p. A2.
34. Ted Baehr, *The Christian Family Guide to Movies and Video,* vol. 1, 1989, p. 12.

Chapter Three
FREE TO SERVE GOD

1. Displayed on a large sign at the entrance to Auschwitz, a former Nazi concentration camp.
2. From a personal conversation with Representative Ray Allen in October, 1994.

Chapter Four
FREE TO LOVE YOURSELF

1. Bruce Olson, *Bruchko*, (Orlando: Creation House, 1978), p. 37.

Chapter Seven
FREE TO USE MONEY

1. World Vision, MARC Publication newsletter, Spring 1994.
2. Ibid.

Chapter Eight
FREE TO CHANGE THE WORLD

1. David Wilkerson, *Set The Trumpet To Thy Mouth* (World Challenge, 1985).
2. William J. Bennett, *The Index of Leading Cultural Indicators*, p. 11.
3. *Focus on the Family* magazine, "In Defense Of A Little Virginity," reprinted in the *Seattle Post-Intelligencer*, 19 May 1993.

Chapter Ten
SIN'S CALLUSES AND CONSEQUENCES

1. Frederick Douglas, born as a slave in 1817, was one of the leading voices against slavery during his time. This quote was part of a speech given on Independence Day in 1852 in Rochester, New York.

Chapter Twelve
HOLY LIVING AND THE COMING REVIVAL

1. Not his real name.
2. Joseph Tracy, *The Great Awakening* (New York: Russell & Russell, first published 1842), p. 8
3. Ibid., p. 12–13.
4. Ibid., p. 161.
5. Ibid., p. 164.
6. Ibid., p. 85.
7. The remark is historically attributed to Benjamin Franklin, a close friend of George Whitefield.
8. Tracy, p. 116.
9. Ibid, p. 130.
10. Ibid., pp. 382–383.
11. Ibid., p. 391.
12. *Focus on the Family* magazine, January 1994.
13. Charles Finney, sermon entitled "The Seared Conscience," published in *The Oberlin Evangelist*, 1865.

Revive America Seminar

A FRESH WIND of God is starting to blow across America. The early rumblings of revival have begun in many towns and cities, schools, and campuses in response to the prayers of God's people. One of the tools God is using is YWAM Renewal Ministries' Revive America Seminar—a weekend experience of cutting edge teaching and prayer, designed to stir hearts, confront apathy, and move the hand of God.

Will you set aside one weekend to allow God to do a work in you and through you?

SPEAKER: Ron Boehme, director of YWAM Renewal Ministries, and one of the leading prophetic voices for spiritual awakening in America.

FORMAT AND FOCUS: Friday evening, all day Saturday, Sunday morning (optional) and evening. Each session includes corporate worship, teaching on revival, and small and large group prayer and application. A twenty-four hour prayer watch for revival will begin, and the weekend experience will conclude with participants being invited to sign a national "Covenant" to pray for revival in America until it comes.

For scheduling a Revive America Seminar, please contact:

YWAM Renewal Ministries
Box 1634
Port Orchard, WA 98366
Ph: (360) 876-3432
Fax: (360) 876-1332
E-mail: GSCV82A@prodigy.com

Other Resources by Ron Boehme

BOOKS

Leadership for the 21st Century: Changing Nations through the Power of Serving

A clarion call for the church to lead the world into the twenty-first century by serving people the way Jesus did—in all the spheres of life. Contains great teaching on Christian world view, how to change and shape nations, the essence and characteristics of servant leadership, and an incredible look into the coming world revival. Great for study groups and personal growth.

If God Has a Plan For My Life, Why Can't I Find It?

Does God really have a plan for my life? Is it really possible to find out what God wants me to do? Can I really live out God's plan for my life? All the answers are a resounding YES! as Ron Boehme clearly shows you how to discover God's will. He then gives you the road map that will enable you to navigate your future with confidence. Essential for YOU (also great as a group study).

TAPES

America's Greatest Need: Revival

In this clear and revealing four-tape series, Ron Boehme strips away the mysteries of spiritual awakening and beckons us to get ready for the coming revival. You'll learn what revival is and how you can prepare for it.

Why Is God Being Merciful to America?

This enlightening four-tape series exposes the four sins of a nation facing terminal judgment from God, showing why revival in America is crucial to fulfilling the Great Commission. It's all part of an amazing end-time plan!

History's Greatest Army: the Church in the 1990s

What is God's message to the Church in the 1990s? In this revealing two-tape series, Ron shares seven characteristics of the global Church in the 1990s that will make us the world's greatest and most triumphant army.

PRODUCTS AVAILABLE FROM:

Renewal Communications
P.O. Box 1634
Port Orchard, WA 98366

Fax: (360) 876-1332
E-mail: GSCV82A@prodigy.com